T0119554

THE

SONGS

OF

ANTÓNIO

BOTTO

EDITED AND WITH AN

INTRODUCTION BY

JOSIAH

BLACKMORE

UNIVERSITY OF

MINNESOTA PRESS

MINNEAPOLIS

LONDON

ANTÓNIO BOTTO

THE

SONGS

OF

ANTÓNIO

Botto

TRANSLATED BY

FERNANDO

PESSOA

Original translation privately printed, 1948

Photographs of António Botto courtesy of Isabel Pontes Boto

Copyright 2010 by the Regents of the University of Minnesota

Published by the University of Minnesota Press
111 Third Avenue South, Suite 290
Minneapolis, MN 55401-2520
http://www.upress.umn.edu

Library of Congress Cataloging-in-Publication Data
Botto, António, 1897–1959.
[Poems. English. Selections]
The songs of António Botto / António Botto ;
translated [from the Portuguese] by Fernando Pessoa ;
edited and with an introduction by Josiah Blackmore.
p. cm.
Original translation privately printed, 1948.
Includes bibliographical references and index.
ISBN 978-0-8166-7100-7 (hc : alk. paper)
ISBN 978-0-8166-7101-4 (pbk. : alk. paper)
1. Botto, António, 1897–1959—Translations into
English. I. Pessoa, Fernando, 1888–1935.
II. Blackmore, Josiah, 1959– III. Title.
PQ9261.B64A2 2010
869.1'42—dc22 2010036995

Printed in the United States of America on acid-free paper

The University of Minnesota is an
equal-opportunity educator and employer.

17 16 15 14 13 12 11 10   10 9 8 7 6 5 4 3 2 1

CONTENTS

The Songs of António Botto are presented here as they appear in the 1948 privately printed *Songs,* translated from the Portuguese by Fernando Pessoa. I have silently corrected the occasional typographical or punctuation error, and spelling has been modified to contemporary American practice. I have let all other aspects of Pessoa's English stand. I restore Pessoa's "Foreword by the Translator," which was not printed in the 1948 volume but is part of Pessoa's typescript of the translations, in two copies, now in the António Botto Archive (Espólio de António Botto) housed in the Biblioteca Nacional, Lisbon (call no. E12/28-28A). A note by Botto accompanying these documents indicates that the translations were complete in 1933. The title page of one typescript announces a preface by M. Teixeira Gomes, "Sometime Portuguese Ambassador at the Court of St. James and President of the Portuguese Republic," presumably an English translation of Gomes's prefatory remarks first printed in the 1930 edition of the *Canções*; that preface, however, is not included in Pessoa's typed pages. Although no place of publication is identified in the 1948 *Songs*, one document in the Botto Archive indicates the book was published in London, while there is also the possibility that the book was printed more than once and for distribution in Brazil: a flyer (call no. E12/2423) states that the *Songs* are "printed now, once again, for distribution to a select elite of São Paulo" (*impresso, de novo, agora, para ser destribuido a uma escolhida elite de São Paulo*).

Botto would periodically issue new editions of the *Canções* until his death (the last one to be published in his lifetime appeared in 1956). In these editions, new poems would be added and older ones sometimes revised. Smaller, individual books of poetry that Botto had published with their own titles (such as *Curiosidades estheticas* or *Olympíadas*) would be incorporated into the successive versions of the *Canções*. Thus no two editions are exactly alike. As the basis of his translations, Pessoa clearly used the 1932 version. There are a number of parallels between it and the *Songs* in terms of the poems included, the order of presentation of the poems, and wording, spacing, and punctuation. It was the last edition published before Pessoa's death in 1935.

António Botto's
Bruises of Light

> And, a long while
> In silence,
> I hear a voice that speaks to me . . .

So writes António Tomaz Botto (1897–1959), a Portuguese
poet who claims a singular place in the literary tradition of his
home country and in modern poetry. Botto's poetic speak-
ing, consolidated in the several editions of his *Canções* (or
"Songs") that stand as his literary signature, breaks a silence
in Portuguese letters in that here, for the first time, is a voice
that speaks openly, frankly, and unapologetically about ho-
mosexual eroticism and sentiment. Botto's is an uninhibited,
often celebratory, firsthand expression of homoerotic en-
counters and experience cast in an attitude and tone of mat-
ter-of-factness that strike a startlingly contemporary chord.
In Anna M. Klobucka's assessment, Botto forged an original
discourse of an unorthodox identity in the context of early

twentieth-century Portuguese modernism, in which the possibility of male same-sex desire is pursued and even taken as a preexisting given.[1] Francisco Salinas Portugal notes that in Botto's world homosexual love is normal while heterosexual love defines the margin of deviation. Botto's enactment of what we might call in current terminology a *queer* self-fashioning demands attention because it adds to the ever more complex place of gay experience and sensibility in the landscapes of modern artistic expression and consciousness.[2]

Botto's *Canções,* when it first appeared in the initial decades of the twentieth century, prompted a number of essays and books by Portuguese thinkers of the time who both vilified and admired it, sometimes simultaneously. In the preface to the 1921 edition, for example, Jayme de Balsemão finds Botto's poetic inspiration to be "noble and daring" (xi); João Gaspar Simões, a luminary of the early twentieth-century Portuguese intelligentsia, notes that Botto was "debated and discussed like few others. . . . in the end, he was accepted and admired like no other modern poet" (*História da poesia* 532); and finally, the literary critic Hernani Cidade remarks of Botto that "no poet . . . makes traditional harmonies and rhythms with such a fine voluptuousness as António Bôto, whose lyrics, even though frequently issuing forth from a filthy spring, never cease to shine in a lustrous wash of perfect form and music" (226).[3] Yet for all of Botto's critical acclaim, and for all of his often hotly contested verse, Botto's oeuvre fell into almost complete oblivion after his death, despite the fact that it was regularly, if infrequently, reprinted.

For years, Botto maintained a friendship and collaboration with Fernando Pessoa (1888–1935), the poet who would emerge as Portugal's preeminent representative of modernism and who is now a cornerstone of the Portuguese literary canon. Pessoa, bilingual in Portuguese and English due to an adolescence spent in Durban, South Africa, held a great esteem for Botto.[4] One of the expressions of that esteem was the formal literary attention paid to Botto's poetry in the form of a translation into English of the *Canções* as *Songs*, completed in 1933 but not printed until 1948 (and then only privately, with no indication of publisher or place of publication), thirteen years after Pessoa's death. Botto considered Pessoa's translations to be "magisterial" (Fernandes, *António Botto* 66), but the print run of the *Songs* must have been very small as today only a handful of copies survive. Apart from its literary merits, Pessoa's translation grants Botto an international accessibility and solidifies his status as one of the principal figures of early twentieth-century Portuguese literary culture.[5] For students and scholars of modern poetry in general, Botto's is an important and urgent voice, and Pessoa's translation allows his voice to be heard outside Portugal. The present volume therefore seeks to participate in the recovery of António Botto for a more global readership. It presents the translations of the 1948 *Songs* and recuperates Pessoa's "Foreword by the Translator" that was not included in the 1948 book. As a testament to the bond Botto and Pessoa shared, the book concludes with a translation into English of Botto's memorial poem to Pessoa, which appeared in the 1941 *Canções,* just six years after Pessoa's death.

António Botto was born in 1897 in rural Casal da Concavada, in the municipality of Abrantes, and beginning in 1902 was a resident with his family of the ancient Moorish quarter of Lisbon known as the Alfama. Botto published the first version of the *Canções* in 1920, titled the *Canções do sul* (Songs of the South), at the age of twenty-three. The young poet frequented literary circles and Lisbon bookshops and was soon part of a group of intellectuals and artists who ushered Portugal into modernity. According to the recollections of some who knew Botto, he made no secret of his homosexuality. L. P. Moitinho de Almeida, for example, recalls the hostile environment in Lisbon following the 1922 edition of the *Canções* and claims that the poet wielded a sardonic wit and had a passion for sailors.[6] In 1924, Botto was posted to a government job in colonial Angola and then returned to Lisbon in 1925 to work for the Civil Government of Lisbon (the same organization that seized the 1922 *Canções*; see below). After eighteen years in government service Botto was dismissed in 1942, without a pension, for lacking "the moral character necessary for carrying out his duties" (quoted in Fernandes, *António Botto* 52).[7] The document in question specifies three reasons for Botto's dismissal: (1) disobeying a direct order from a superior; (2) failure to maintain an appropriate professional composure and dignity by directing flirtatious comments to a colleague, comments that "demonstrate tendencies condemned by social morality"; and (3) writing and reciting poetry during business hours, an activity impairing proper office discipline. After his short stint in Africa, Botto continued his literary activities and contributed to newspapers and magazines through the 1940s.

In 1947, disillusioned with life in Portugal and the often vitriolic criticism of his work, Botto emigrated to Brazil with his wife, Carminda da Conceição Silva Rodrigues Botto, and took up residence for four years in São Paulo. He moved to Rio de Janeiro in 1951. In São Paulo, Botto hosted a weekly radio show, was active in literary clubs and gave poetry recitations, and earned the friendship of Carlos Drummond de Andrade, a major poet of Brazilian modernism. Yet, as in Portugal, Botto's life in Brazil was made difficult by critics, and near the end he became ill and underwent hospitalization. While in Brazil, Botto decided to spell his surname with only one *t* because, as he wrote in a letter to George Lucas, manager of the Bertrand Bookstore in Lisbon, "two t's weigh too heavily on me" (quoted in Fernandes, *António Botto* 34). Botto never abandoned hope of returning to Portugal but did not live to realize this hope. He was struck by a car on March 4, 1959, in Copacabana and died thirteen days later. His remains were returned to Portugal in 1965.

In May 1922, the second, expanded edition of Botto's *Canções* appeared, published by Fernando Pessoa's own Editora Olisipo (Olisipo Press). This book cemented Botto's reputation as a poet of note, if also as a poet of controversy, since it ignited a short-lived but intense polemic generally referred to as the "literature of Sodom." The controversy began in July 1922 when Pessoa published an essay titled "António Botto e o ideal estético em Portugal" (António Botto and the aesthetic ideal in Portugal) in the arts magazine *Contemporânea*. Here, Pessoa makes a complex argument claiming that Botto "is the only Portuguese, of those known to be writing today, to whom the label of aesthete may be applied without question" (121). In the next issue of the same magazine, the journalist Álvaro Maia published a response to Pessoa's essay called "Literatura de Sodoma" (Literature of Sodom), a diatribe against Pessoa, Botto, and homosexuality couched in religious rhetoric. At one point he asks, implicitly referring to Botto, if "those individuals who, pathologically, swerve away from the contemplation of masculine beauty and let themselves be borne away by the loathsome tide of perverted desire, are by chance aesthetes, in the pure and unadulterated meaning of the word?" (57). In the same paragraph,

Maia states that the kind of beauty at issue in Botto is nothing more than the "temptation toward abnormal sexuality." Maia's article in turn led the philosopher Raul Leal (under the pseudonym Henoch) to publish a small booklet called *Sodoma divinizada* (Sodom deified), printed by Pessoa's Olisipo Press in 1923. This work, though beginning with references to Maia's article (which Leal strongly condemns) and to Botto's poetry, is in fact an extended exposition of Leal's own brand of religious philosophy, which he calls "transcendent vertiginism." *Sodoma divinizada* explains, in sometimes contorted fashion, how *luxúria* (licentiousness) and *pederastia* (pederasty) are "divine works."

Leal's pamphlet infuriated a Catholic student contingent in Lisbon, and the result was the formation of a Students of Lisbon Action League, championed by Pedro Teotónio Pereira, who would later become part of António de Oliveira Salazar's dictatorial regime, the Estado Novo (New State). In a move bent on cleansing Lisbon of its moral putrefaction, the league published a notice in a newspaper in which it reprimands the Civil Government for allowing certain books to be sold, books for which "it's difficult to say what's most repugnant and base about them—their disgraceful language or the shamelessness of their authors" (quoted in Leal 89). These books, in the league's words, contain "heinous pornography" (89). Shortly thereafter, in a type of inquisitorial gesture, the government confiscated and burned copies of

Botto's *Canções*, Leal's booklet, and *Decadência* (Decadence), a book of poetry by the lesbian poet Judith Teixeira (1880–1959). These publications reputedly continued to be sold under the counter. But as R. W. Howes points out, the scandal had no lasting effect since Botto continued to publish under Salazar's dictatorship ("Fernando Pessoa" 165).

The uproar might explain the replacement in some copies of the 1922 *Canções* of the photograph of the bare-shouldered Botto (Figure 1) with a more staid portrait (Figure 2). In the first photo, Botto's relationship with the camera, and implicitly with the reader, is remarkable, and it challenges visual representations of masculinity and heterosexual desire. The poet's attitude is relaxed and insouciant. The languorous, provocative posture suggests self-possession, an almost defiant gesture of unencumbered, self-aware indulgence in bodily pleasure in keeping with the topic of many of the poems contained in the pages to follow. The voluptuary air of the photo draws the reader into the sensuality of the *Canções*, an air dramatized by the chiaroscuro contrast. Botto is both active in his fixed, knowing, and centered gaze on the lens/spectator and, with the entreating tilt of the head and glimpse of shirtless torso, and also passive, an image of fem-

FIGURE 1. The photograph of Botto that appears
in the second edition (1922) of the *Canções*.
This edition ignited the literature of Sodom polemic.

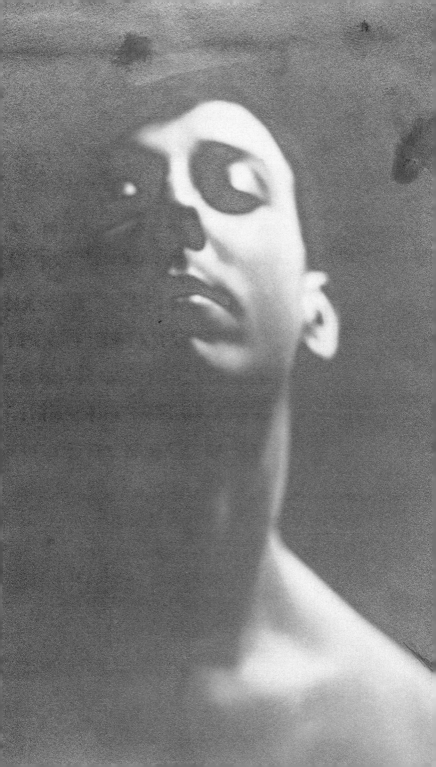

inine receptivity. This portrait, we might say, draws on the aesthetics of desire in visual culture first expressed by Johann Joachim Winckelmann (1717–68), commonly regarded as the founder of art history and whose selected words on male beauty serve as an epigraph to all editions of the *Canções* beginning with the 1930 printing. James M. Saslow notes that in Winckelmann's valuing of the androgynous male as beautiful, "men could now play both the desiring spectator and the vulnerable recipient of that desiring look" (160). Even if not androgynous, Botto here seems to inhabit just such a zone of the shifting positionalities and vectors of desire.

The central place of aesthetics and eroticism in the contemporary reception of Botto's 1922 edition requires us to comment, however briefly, on Pessoa's essay on the aesthetic ideal in Botto that was the opening salvo in the 1922–23 dispute, both for what it says and does not say. In a nutshell, Pessoa makes an argument claiming that Botto is an aesthete, the only writer worthy of that label, because he pursues a Hellenic ideal in his poetry. Hellenic civilization, according to Pessoa, is at its essence artistic, based on the premise

FIGURE 2. The more staid photograph of the poet that appears in some copies of the 1922 *Canções* (possibly as a replacement of the more provocative photograph seen in Figure 1) and in *Ódio e amor* (Hatred and love, 1947).

that to create art is to make the world more beautiful. Within this artistic frame the activity of the artist is intellectual, since it is consciously employed. Botto's treatment of male beauty, in Pessoa's formulation, is entirely intellectual, entirely thought-driven. Sexuality, Pessoa observes, is an instinct "normally directed toward the opposite sex" (129), and the female body as an object of artistic representation possesses only gracefulness (*graça*), while the masculine body unites both gracefulness and strength and therefore exemplifies a higher attainment of beauty. The masculine body is the preferred object of contemplation by the aesthete, who is guided by beauty and not by the "animal aesthetic" (129) of sexuality. And although Pessoa acknowledges that Botto's poems are in fact a "hymn to pleasure" (131), they are so only in an intellectual fashion and hence are neither moral nor immoral. Botto's version of pleasure, for Pessoa, "does not awaken the joy of life" (131). In another essay published ten years later in the first edition of Botto's *Cartas que me foram devolvidas* (Letters returned to me), Pessoa further argues that the aesthete adores beauty only contemplatively, and not through action: "The aesthetic ideal excludes the moral ideal, since the moral ideal is born of action. . . . The aesthete, then, would be he whose ideal of beauty is free from the attraction to life or to the opposite sex" ("António Botto e o ideal estético creador" 128).

Pessoa's arguments, especially in the 1922 essay, are complex and often turgid. So much so that, in the opinion of Anna Klobucka and Mark Sabine, Pessoa's analysis of Botto and homosexuality may be a bit tongue-in-cheek:

> Anything beyond the most superficial inspection of Pessoa's supposed critical appreciation of Botto's work reveals it as an arch and supercilious riposte to the self-appointed moral guardians who first condemned the young poet. It bamboozles the uninitiated with rarified erudition and convoluted logic, while sending a very different encoded message to those familiar either with Botto and his flamboyantly advertised sexual identity or with the euphemistic currency of the epithets "aesthetic" and "Hellenic" in the works of Pater and the circle of British critics, scholars, and social activists that first coalesced around him. . . . Thus Pessoa advances a characteristically polyvalent justification of homoerotism as literary topos without venturing a committed defence of homosexual agency itself. (15)

What Klobucka and Sabine point to here is the more-than-apparent gap between what Pessoa claims is Botto's governing poetic principle and the evidence of the poetry itself. Far from being intellectually removed or contemplative, or solely turning on an abstract, Hellenic "aesthetic ideal," Botto's *Songs* present an intense and personal immersion in the ecstasy and sometimes resulting emotional anguish of homoerotic encounter that is anything but abstract.[8] The personal voice that speaks evokes a world of intensely lived, firsthand experience; even if such experiences are not Botto's own biographical experiences, they are meant to suggest lived experience, lived contact—deeply erotic, sensual, and self-aware.[9] In this, Botto's homoerotic poetry shares an affinity with C. P. Cavafy's; as Keith Taylor observes, apropos of Daniel Mendelsohn's translations, Cavafy's "poems seem to be very quiet, yet are filled with a painful longing. They have the ambience, the atmosphere, of desire." To subsume the variety and complexity of erotic and emotional experience as recorded in the *Songs* under the rubric of the aesthetic ideal is to diminish the poetry it contains and the singularity of Botto's poetic voice.[10] Like Winckelmann, whose "eroticism and aesthetics [were] intimately connected" (Aldrich 49), so too Botto, who embraced the aesthetic not as an end in itself but as an available platform for the expression of a homo-erotic self.[11] Hellenic civilization and art, as Callón Torres suggests (70), may have served as one way to legitimate ex-plorations of homosexuality.

As an important voice in modern poetry, the modernist movement, and the gay canon, Botto raises several topics of interest for the general reader and literary studies scholar. My intention in the remaining space of this introduction is simply to tag a few of these issues and offer some interpretive comments, a kind of introit to reading Botto. Not all poems in the *Songs* and in the several editions of the *Canções* pub-lished over the decades, it must be noted, turn on homoeroti-cism, although it is what most consistently defines the voice we hear. António Botto's *Songs* induct the reader into a world of intense eroticism and emotion, expressed in an accessible and limpid poetic idiom, a language that characteristically structures words, verses, and stanzas with a certain musicality, a certain pulse. The title *Songs* evokes the cadences and metrical simplicity of traditional Portuguese poetry and folk verses that appealed to many modernist poets—in fact, one of Pessoa's own collections of poetry bears the title *Cancioneiro* (Songbook)—as it is also heir to the musically oriented compositions of late nineteenth-century Symbolist poetry.

Botto is a poet of physical and emotional desire, a poet of the male body. His literary voice is confessional, personal, intimate, one that revels and luxuriates in moments of eroticism; this voice equally expresses an aching awareness of the impossibility of love and lasting connection. Botto speaks of silence and suffering, of love and desire in all their contradictions, and of being forced to be someone other than himself. The encounters with lovers are transient; while there is an exquisite indulgence in another's body, kiss, or embrace, in the fleshly and sentimental realms of homosexual pleasure and emotion, the poetic scenarios are typically set in darkness, shadow, or failing, crepuscular light. A sense of resignation and the inevitability of aging and death courses through the *Songs*. These poems speak softly of melancholy while they also extol and celebrate the male form.

As a Portuguese poet, from a culture historically inspired

and influenced by the sea, Botto feels an affinity with the ocean. In "I heard throughout yesterday" the sea itself rises up and sings, another male body that has become a siren and entices the poet into its depths.[12] Botto's poetic cadences are wave-like, like the unceasing ocean beat of breakers on the shore, pulling the reader into a rhythm of approach and withdrawal, of epiphanic moments of bodily and emotional encounter that presage dissipation—a music of passion, exchanged glances, and a longing for what will never be. Yet there is also a vitality to these poems, a vitality that emanates from the celebration of topics such as youth, athleticism, or moments of fevered, intense engagements that satisfy the psyche's and body's appetites. The *Songs* are at once a testament to hidden or suppressed desire and to desire's already realized dailiness.

Consider some examples. "No, let us kiss, only kiss," the composition that initiates the 1930 *Canções* and remains at the front of all subsequent versions as the book's flagship lyric, establishes motifs that Botto will regularly repeat. It begins with a stark, hortatory "No," and we surmise the question that lingers just prior to the poet's first word, an erotic proposition that moves the poet to speak to his lover and in so doing restricts an intimate encounter to a mere kiss. It betrays a desire on the part of the unseen and unheard companion for a more involved contact. The poet's denial is at once a refusal of pleasure but also its enticing deferral. This inaugural negation, this erotically freighted abstinence, gives voice to the *Songs*; it mobilizes a postponement of want that at times will be urgently, even ecstatically, overruled. To deny physical consummation is to affirm and value it, a sort of tonal counterpoint in the poet's voice that sets personal yearning against the possibility of lasting fulfillment, a tension at the heart of Botto's poetic personality. The next lines are "Keep / For some better moment / Your manly body so brown"; judging from the use of the adjective *brown*, the poet is presumably describing the body of a swarthy companion, perhaps of a field laborer or worker tanned by the Portuguese sun. The waning, golden light of late afternoon suffuses the intimate space of the poem and suggests a certain resignation. The dying light exteriorizes the withholding and hesitation in the poet's voice. But *brown* (Portuguese *trigueiro*, which can as well mean tan or golden) could also imply bronze; Botto, in this possibility, infers a statuesque body, a personal engagement with the sculpted but distant bodies of athletes we find elsewhere in the poems, such as in "Olympiads." Botto appropriates a "classical" body into his private world, and here is an example where the outer form of male beauty so prized by Hellenic culture becomes part of a much more intimate discourse. The poem ultimately moves from the initial "no" to the closing "yes," a movement from negation to affirmation.

The denied or deferred erotic yearnings of the opening

poem find a counterpart in the realization of such yearnings expressed in others. But the realizations of pleasure often carry with them the shadow of Thanatos. "Listen, my angel" records a feverishness of kissing (Botto's preferred mode of physical connection); kisses and passionate embraces in the dark occupy the next poem ("Who is it that clasps me to him") as well. These gestures are part of a gradual death and melting away, a dissipation, "like a vague scent in the air." In a few significant instances, Botto expresses the irrational, ineffable delirium of physical contact and physical love through religious imagery and allusion. "The night" and "The moon" are good examples. In "The night" there is a sensuality to night and death that attends the scene of frenetic, erotic encounter. "And I, clasped within your arms, / Almost dreamt that I was dead" construes the poet's relation to his lover as a kind of pietà. A luxuriousness to death and mourning exists alongside moments of carnal satisfaction that border on the sacramental. Botto employs an idiom, saturated with sensuality and the plenitude of the senses, that evinces religious rapture. The pronoun *he*, referring to the poet's lover, is capitalized in the original ("Ele," line 21), a move that invests the lover with a religious power and melds him with the Christ on the crucifix who supervises the scene. "The flesh of the rankest sinner / Is like the flesh of the saint," Botto writes in "Listen, my angel," where sinner and saint are both subject to ecstatic, irrational surrender, to oneiric states of frenzy that overwhelm the body. "The night" ends with the arrival of the sun as the lovers passionately kiss, like the coming of the dawn that surprises paramours in medieval *albas*. "The moon," in which the cloak of darkness protects the tryst and the moon rides high, ends with a Dionysian immersion in wine. Botto's wine is Bacchic and pagan while it is also the wine of communion that marks the joining of two bodies. This wine allows escape from pain—it quiets the lion that clutches at the heart in "Blessèd be thou"—since it is like the waters of Lethe, causing oblivion and forgetfulness.

The inebriation that closes "The moon" follows the poet's remark on releasing the body "I had so madly kissed, / So unconsciously." The expression Pessoa translates as "unconsciously" is, in Botto's Portuguese, *sem sentir*, literally, "without feeling (it)." The locution raises the possibility of the poet's alienation from himself, from his own body and sensations, and speaks to a sort of existential angst. A similar idea appears in "No, let us kiss, only kiss": "living too much too near you / Has changed me, I am another . . ." The tension between the indulgence of bodily pleasure that occurs "without feeling" or "unconsciously" in "The moon" and the total surrender to the sensual, bodily dialogue between lovers in "What really hurts me" ("Our bodies understand each other. That is enough.") is never entirely resolved and characterizes the conflicted position of the aware, homosexual self in a time and a society that stifle this mode of being.

The internal divide, the dissociated selves residing within the poetic voice, is perhaps most evident in "Boy," Pessoa's translation of Botto's "Adolescente" (adolescent), a word that connotes an awakening into sexuality and maturity. The entrance into adulthood makes references to death all the more poignant and speaks of an already jaded youth. In some sense the boy is already gone, already dead in the perspective of the poet who writes in later years. Botto regularly mourns the loss of youth and beauty, "the pity of my decay!" ("I have no longer any pride"). In another poem, he simply declares, "I am dead" ("I am glad, I really am").

There is a steady procession of bodies throughout the pages of the *Songs*—bodies of lovers, of the poet, of athletes. And then there is a dramatic moment when the body of a dancing woman appears, an exception to the male-dominated world of physicality and an apparent pause in the narrative of homoerotic desire. This moment occurs in "Lovely, golden." We might read the Orientalized female dancer, whose exposed body is described in some detail, as a spectacle of feminine desire meant to solidify the intense, homoerotic ambience of the *Songs* rather than interrupt it.[13] If we assume a male spectator, identified by the poet's interjection "Dance, my child, dance!," then we can locate here a male gaze constituted by the viewers of the dance that triangulates desire between men through the woman and allows for a homosocial-homosexual continuum of the kind Eve Kosofsky Sedgwick explores in *Between Men*.[14] Next to the bodies of the exotic others such as Salome and the sexualized Africans in "Many voices," the body of the poet himself is also a spectacle, a repository of erotic memory, as we see in "No, this isn't jealousy": "I know your nerves very well: / They have left stains of their fire / In my flesh so nicely brown." Pessoa translates Botto's *nódoas de lume* as "stains of their fire," an expression that might also be translated as "bruises of light." These *nódoas*, a sensorial memory on skin the hue of waning light, are like the rapidly fading memory of a touch. The body pleasurably remembers and retains the sense of contact with the body of another, but in a way that aches. The evaporation of pleasure compares to a present darkness or melancholy, and the remnant of this process is the poem. "The rest is literature," Botto writes, modifying Hamlet's dying words, as if to say that after the contact that imprints the body with a bruising, evanescent light, all that is left is poetry as a monument to what once was. In this poem, Botto eschews what might be construed as the more trivial or banal emotion of jealousy to speak of something deeper when he sees his lover with a woman, a "sorrow" that recognizes a more profound deceit in his lover's heterosexual alliance. What appears to be a misogynistic sentiment in

Botto's declaration "That woman / Is never worthy of you" is perhaps the frustrated result of living in a homophobic society that ignores the possibility of homoerotic connection. "I have left my love forever. / I have done what the world wants," Botto writes in surrender and resignation ("I sought in the painful longing").

Botto's relegation of women to the periphery of male physicality dominant in these poems appears again in "The morning is full of light" ("Olympiads") where the poet exalts the sculpted bodies of the Marathon runners whose "Holy flesh" is "Without the taint / Of any woman's embrace." Here is one instance where we might find, at least partially, the Hellenic, artistic ideal advocated by Pessoa. The body of the athlete, in this reading, would not be tainted by sexual contact with a woman, which in Pessoa's argument defines the "animal instinct"; at the end of the poem, however, the athlete receives a woman's embrace, although how willingly is not clear. The chaste body of the athlete here may stand as a model of a body untouched by sexual commerce and, in this sense, would represent a purity of aesthetic form detached from the world of the flesh. If we accept Pessoa's argument in this instance, it is important to repeat that this abstract, bodily ideal does not characterize all of Botto's poems, or even the majority of them. The poems of "Small Sculptures" and "Olympiads" perhaps most strongly establish a formal aesthetic of male beauty, although not unavoidably in the terms laid out by Pessoa. The primacy of male beauty in art as espoused by Winckelmann in the epigraph to Botto's book does not necessarily claim an erotic basis to this beauty, but as noted above, Aldrich (49) argues that Winckelmann's aesthetics and erotics overlapped. Walter Pater, in his seminal book *The Renaissance*,[15] also cites the Winckelmann passage used by Botto; Heather Love ("Forced Exile") explores the possibility of a queer Pater and the relationship between his marginalized sexuality and his aesthetics. It perhaps should come as no surprise that Botto dedicates one of his poems to Pater.[16]

Whatever disinterested aesthetic ideal might underlie the valuing of the male form, it is important to note that the appraisals of athletic male beauty are often shot through with emotional or impassioned responses to the bodies described. This situates Botto in the tradition of Winckelmann and Pater. Winckelmann's descriptions of classical sculptures, for example, are also marked by close attention to their physicality with words that are effusive and emotional (Aldrich 50), while Pater "attempted to carve out a mental territory for formerly forbidden passions, to exempt the lust for physical beauty in art, or in life, from rational scrutiny or moral judgment" (Saslow 184). Botto's occasional separation of the erotic and the aesthetic may, in part, explain his repudiation or disavowing of the erotic as a love that is "degrading, very vile" ("It's a pity, but I must not understand you"). But even in this instance the recourse to a denied, physical relation with his male addressee might also emphasize Botto's perceived futility or impossibility of lasting connection, a pessimism evident in the observation that "all . . . leads to nothing." While the aesthetic and the intimate, erotic sensibilities of the poet can sometimes be distinct, the tension between external beauty and the private impulses of the poetic voice surfaces. There is in Botto a complicated fluidity between the visual and the visceral, between outer form and inner life.

The erotic and emotional experiences in the *Songs* define what in contemporary parlance may be termed a gay voice or sensibility, keeping in mind that *gay* and *queer* carry a number of connotations not easily or transparently applicable to the past or to cultures outside the Anglo-American environment in which they were developed.[17] In Botto's time the designation of homosexuality differentiated a sector of the population as possessed of a pathological condition. In Portugal several sexological works were published in the early twentieth century, chief among them Arlindo Camillo Monteiro's *Amor sáfico e socrático* (Sapphic and Socratic love). This book, which evidently took the inspiration for its title from Magnus Hirschfeld's first publication on homosexuality, *Sappho and Socrates*, appeared in 1922, precisely the year of publication of Botto's second, scandal-inducing edition of the *Canções*. Monteiro's book was published under the legal and nosological auspices of the Institute of Legal Medicine of Lisbon and announces on its cover that it is *"para uso de letrados e bibliotecas"* (for the use of scholars and libraries), presumably to establish the book's contents as a serious work meant for detached, scientific inquiry and to discourage its consultation by prurient readers. Monteiro gives a lengthy history of homosexuality, which he deems, overall, a "sexual anomaly." In Stefan Schukowski's argument, Pessoa may have concentrated on Botto's aestheticism in his 1922 essay in a move to save Botto from this pathologizing perception by claiming that Botto was talking about male beauty in his poetry and not homosexuality.

In the Portuguese context, Eduardo Pitta argues that there is a difference between gay literature and homosexual literature, the former a result of post-Stonewall culture that always manifests an ideological substratum; because of this, Pitta claims, there is no *gay* Portuguese author (*Fractura* 29).[18] Without calling Pitta's definition into question, we could also say that Botto's awareness of his sexuality is itself a mark of self-definition. Botto is like Cavafy, who in Gregory Woods's analysis "chose to write *as* a homosexual, with homosexual desires" (187, emphasis in original). Botto hence occupies a place in the flux and flow of homosexual or gay literary subjectivities of the modern period. And while we need to exercise caution in the application of words, terms, and categories in scholarly endeavors, sometimes critical debates that focus too much on terminology can get us caught up in the intricacies of language that end up suffocating voices that speak to us from a distance. One aspect of Botto's striking modernity is his sensitivity to the often deleterious effects of categorization and labeling, so that if we are to take the following lines from "What is it that the spring murmurs?" as any indication, Botto poetically proclaims the urgency of liberation from labels:

> Live only at the mercy of sensation.
>
> To define ourselves
> Is simply to curtail
> The soul
> And to close our understanding.

Given the historical particulars of the time, we might read these lines on one level as a rejection of the pathologization of homosexuality or "deviant" sexuality, a slap in the face to modern medicalizations of erotic impulses, certain forms of emotional attachment, and their attendant ways of life and being.

Is it possible, then, to discern a queer voice emanating from the *Songs*? I believe it is. While it is, on the one hand, necessary to acknowledge that alternate forms of sexuality and eroticism, including homosexuality, were common in fin de siècle literature, on the other hand we must also recognize that Botto wrote on the chronological end of this period of European literary history and from within an avowedly "modern" culture. The homoerotic element in Botto's poetry is much more than a literary vogue—it witnesses something more transcendent and permanent.[19] The traversal and representation of several states of physical and emotional experience, the multiplicity of encounters, misunderstandings, and unrequited love or passion with remembered lovers contribute collectively to a poetic, first-person subject. Several of the poems of "Boy" begin as if in answer to a question or statement from the poet's lover-interlocutor. These responses establish implicit dialogues with their fictional addressees and consolidate a speaking subject, a unified and proclaimed sense of self. Botto seeks a space for the lyric, gay self; if, as John Emil Vincent argues, lyric is the queerest of genres (xiv), and if lyric is the predominant genre of what we now call a "gay tradition" in literature (Woods 1), then Botto deserves our literary and scholarly attentions and commands an important place in that tradition. In his poetry António Botto, as well as writers like Judith Teixeira, sketches a queer self that speaks clearly, on its own terms, from its own sensibility, across a number and variety of poems. There is, therefore, a queer current in Portuguese modernism. The array of poems in the *Songs* allows us to identify a sustained, poetic project and the emergence of a voice rather than just a literary or poetic treatment of a particular theme. Botto's many poems, and varying contexts and modes of the voice we hear speaking, construct a subject position that was not there before. Botto's continual reissuing of new and expanded versions of the *Canções* contributes as well to the creation and regular reaffirmation of a unified, poetic subject. A presiding consciousness becomes evident as the several individual books of poetry are collected under the title *Canções*. While Fernando Pessoa, with his various heteronyms, was exploring the possibilities of being "plural like the universe," as he once famously wrote, António Botto was promoting another, sole voice, a perceiving, poetic self who claims a place in the world and in the sempiternal flow of human emotion and possibility.

JOSIAH BLACKMORE

THE

SONGS

OF

ANTÓNIO

BOTTO

António Botto, though young, is one of the best-known Portuguese poets of today. His initial success, as anyone who reads these poems can understand, was a succès de scandale. But he quickly came into his own as something more than the poet who had that sort of success.

His peculiar distinction lies in the subtlety, both expressional and rhythmical, with which he deals with thoughts and feelings that are in themselves never complex. This has made him clear to the general public and dear to the literary one.

Whatever else might be said is sufficiently expressed in Senhor Teixeira Gomes's critical preface.[1] And it should be noted that, apart from having been Portuguese Ambassador at the Court of St. James and President of the Portuguese Republic, Senhor Manuel Teixeira Gomes is a subtle critic, both of letters and of art, and one of the greatest present-day writers of Portuguese prose. I stress this because, after all, it is, for our immediate case, the real and truer title.

My translation has been made in the most perfect possible conformity, both expressional and rhythmical, with the original text. This does not mean that the translation is, expressionally and rhythmically, a line-by-line one, though in many cases indeed it is. But I know the poet and the man so well that even when I have changed I have not altered. I have done my best to have these poems set down in English in the poet's exact style and rhythm, as if he had written them in the language.

There are three points in the poems that require explanation, since they involve strictly Portuguese things, which most English readers would naturally be unacquainted with.

The first point refers to popular Portuguese poetry, the suggestions of which underlie, so to speak, in their simplicity and type of emotion, the subtlety of António Botto's poems. Popular Portuguese poetry is all in seven-syllable quatrains, which the poet himself often writes, inserting them here and there in the generally irregular rhythm of his poems, where the sudden popular regularity brings in a curious contrast. As a matter of fact, and apart from quatrains themselves, seven-syllable lines are constantly recurring in these poems.

The second point is the word *Fado*, which is the title of one poem in part VII.[2] I have left the word in the original Portuguese because in the particular sense or senses in which it is here used it is untranslatable. Apart from this, it figures only in the title; I have managed what I think an adequate substitution in the text. The word itself means fate, being derived directly from the Latin *fatum*. In its popular Portuguese use it means, however, two other things. It means, in the first place, prostitution. When a Portuguese woman says, "I am in the fate" (*Ando no fado*), she means that she earns her living as a prostitute. The word also means a slow, sad popular song, originating in or taken to heart by the low quarters of Lisbon. These songs refer generally to the life of prostitutes and of their *amants de coeur*, who are frequently sailors. In António Botto's poem—put into the mouth of a sailor and dealing with prostitution—the word may be said to have both the popular senses.

The third point is the reference to António Nobre in the fourteenth poem of the first part.[3] António Nobre was a remarkable Portuguese poet of the end of the nineteenth century; he died of consumption at the age of thirty-three. He wrote one celebrated book, *Só* (Alone), and another, of lesser note, was published after his death. His poetry is full of sadness and depression, which, though not typical, are certainly distinctively Portuguese. His influence was very great and, as anyone will understand, not always favorable. This will explain why, in an orgy, someone, lighting on his book *Só,* tore it up.[4]

It should be added, in concluding, that António Botto is not only a poet but also the author of two delightful books of tales for children and a dramatist of distinction. He has written, till now, two plays. One, called *Alfama* (the name of a low quarter of Lisbon), deals with a typical aspect of life in that part of the city. The other, *António,* handles in a sad, subtle, and dignified way a case of frustrated homosexual love.

FERNANDO PESSOA, 1933

As it is confessedly the beauty of man which is to be conceived under one general idea, so I have noticed that those who are observant of beauty only in women, and are moved little or not at all by the beauty of men, seldom have an impartial, vital, inborn instinct for beauty in art. To such persons the beauty of Greek art will ever seem wanting, because its supreme beauty is rather male than female.

WINCKELMANN

I

Boy

No, let us kiss, only kiss
In this evening's agony.

Keep
For some better moment
Your manly body so brown.

My desire has now no flame,
And living too much too near you
Has changed me, I am another . . .

The mist of the night comes down.

I can now hardly distinguish
The dark blondness of your hair,
Oh, how beautiful you are!

Death
Should be
Just some vague fancy . . .

Give me your arm. Do not let
Your voice grow so faint and sore.

Yes, let us kiss, only kiss.
Do we need anything more?

2

The night,
How it came in!,
Warm, soft,
Very white, stumbling along,
With the vagueness that it shed;
And I, clasped within your arms,
Almost dreamt that I was dead.

And I saw
Pinks and carnations in heaps;
A Christ on the crucifix:
In your eyes
Softness and coldness together;
Purple damask crushed and soiled,
Sordid hands tearing out music
From the strings of a guitar,
A half-light, candles aglow,
Incense, gold, some sadness far:
And I dying, dying slow . . .

And oh, your little brown face
And the loveliness it has!—

It was more calm than before,
It was tearless, it was dry.
Only your frail body's pose,
Your graceful body's pose was
In mourning, I know not why.

Then wildly, blindly,
I sought your mouth,
Your mouth so healthy and gay,
And we kissed madly and madly . . .
It was day.

And our bodies, clasped and tense,
Like bodies without a sense,
Rolled on the floor . . ., and there was no more . . .

3

The moon
Was wandering in the sky
With the stars that round her loom.

In candelabra
Of bronze
Candles were burning
In the stillness of my room.

On the floor, crumpled in flood,
The velvets seemed
Waves of wine and waves of blood.

He looked at me and he dreamed:
And I
Just smoked in silence and watched
How the white and naked moon
Passed through the skies which it matched.

He came to me, and he sought
Wildly, hungrily and thirstily

My mouth, which he kissed and drained—
My mouth which is like a flower—
And from kissing back refrained.

He drew me towards himself
And, leaning upon my shoulder,
Spoke to me of a fair page
Who had died of love and longing,
Singing, singing, by the sea . . .

I looked at the sky.

The moon was going astray
Among clouds which made the night
Dark and gray.

Then our mouths met in a kiss,
A nervous kiss slowly sinned . . .
Man is driven by desire
As a cloud is by the wind.

Morn was still far, far away.

At last,
Releasing
That body

Which had tired itself to sleep
And I had so madly kissed,
So unconsciously, so well,
I drank wine till all was mist,
I drank wine until I fell.

4

Blessèd be thou,
My true comfort,
My true friend!

When the shadows, when the night
Droop down from the distant sky,
My sorrow
Tremblingly wakes from its sleep.

It is a lion whose art
Is biting slowly and deep
Into the flesh of my heart.

I sing and I weep in pain,
But my sorrow is again
As it was . . .

Then,
Feverish, almost mad, I seek
Oh blessèd wine, your repose;
And my sorrow sleeps at last
And the lion's eyelids close.

I drink more: he sleeps the more.
Ah, it is thou, blessèd wine,
That art the way and the power!

I say to you, souls who bleed,
Sad souls whose life is a wound,
I shall be always
Drunk, drunk, early or late . . .

What a grand life!
To have wine for my own lover
And death for my constant mate!

5

Listen, my angel:
What if I should kiss your skin,
What if I should kiss your mouth
Which is all honey within?

He wanted to move away,
Half in disdain, smiling faint;
But, alas!,
The flesh of the rankest sinner
Is like the flesh of the saint.

Mildly, softly, in a posture
Which was mysteriously feigned,
He gave me his golden body
Which my feverish kisses drained.

In the windowpane the rain
Tinkled lightly, tinkled slow . . .

He clasped me and closed his eyes,
The better to see me there;
And I died, I slowly died,
Like a vague scent in the air . . .

6

Who is it that clasps me to him
In the half-light of my bed?
Who is it that kisses me
And bit my breast till it bled?
Who is it that speaks of death
In my ear, so slow, so sweet?
It is you, lord of my eyes,
Who have my dreams at your feet.

7

Do you see?
Fate came to part us.
We must obey.

Some hidden hand
Has broken—and we did not feel it—
The bond
That bound us two.

Why was that so?
Whom could I ask
Whose any answer would do?

I do not know if I am glad,
If I should laugh
Or weep.

Really, there are such things
In the useless life we keep

That it is best to accept them
This way,
Silently, indifferently,
Just as if we were asleep.

8

I am quite sure
That all between us is over.
Nothing good can last forever
And my good has run to cover.

Oh, don't raise again your arms
Just to clasp again, again,
My silken flesh!

I am leaving you forever.

If some day you should remember
My eyes and their drowsy bronze
And my frail body you knew,
Bring calm
To the sensual thing in you
By drinking wine and by singing
Those verses I sent you once—
That evening, when all was gray . . .

Good-bye!

Those who stay behind may suffer.
Ah, but those who go away!

9

I am glad, I really am,
That you lied
And never came.

But
I must tell you—
Because just telling the truth
Is a sort of talk with God—
When I opened your last letter
I really thought you would come.

First
I felt at home
In the vague unpleasantness
That bit me all—
A clear bite, a raging bite,
Limpid and almost immoral.
Then,
Carefully, upon my hair
I spilt scent,
The most sensual I could get;

And the ache of looking lovely
Pressed me close and made me fret.

From my shoulders Florentine
The precious stones
Ran
Like a river over me,
With a cold luminous beauty.
On my hands, which are so white,
The emeralds gleamed green and bright;
And the pearls
On my arms
Seemed to speak . . .
My hair, all in disorder,
Fell in full waves on my brow
Which was slightly in the shadow
Now.

Always pale, and you would say
That this paleness made the greater
The great beauty that I had.

Over my lips, like a wave,
A smile passed, and it was sad.

The vague night was drawing in.

At last,
Heavily, wearily,
As if I foresaw already
The failure that was to be,
I brought my full body nearer
To that lovely crystal mirror
Whose frame is of ivory.

An adorned corpse—
No longer
The body of that fair boy,
That frail and beautiful boy,
That you kissed so many times!

Weaker, sadder,
I let tears come,
And in the shadow I fell
Into a dream of remembering
The dream of you I had shed.

I am glad, I really am,
That you lied and never came.

Stay away, love!
                    I am dead.

1 0

No, this isn't jealousy.
It's sorrow,
A sorrow
That tears my heart to confusion.

That woman
Is never worthy of you;
She does not live in your life,
She cannot fit the illusion
Your sensuality creates.
But she is lovely, you say;
And I say that you are wrong.

Beauty
Was always
Just a secondary thing
In the body that we love.
There is no beauty at all.
Anyhow, it can't endure.
Beauty
Is no more than the desire

[29]

That makes our weary heart move.
The rest is literature.

I know your nerves very well:
They have left stains of their fire
In my flesh so nicely brown,
In this flesh
That looked like the light of autumn
And now slowly goldens down
To an end nothing can soften.

Don't I know your sex so well?
Have you not liked me so often?

The fresh pressure of your kiss,
The power of your embrace—
 All that I have deeply tried . . .

No, this isn't jealousy.
But, when I saw you with her—
No one was looking—, I cried.

1 1

You say you're coming, and then
I just get letters,
Words,
And the petal of a pink
Which was lovely when it was.

Disillusion me. I'm strong.

I wish to give myself,
To feel
Another body that means
Really to become mine,
To vibrate,
To make all its life my own,
Nor to be as you have been,
A bodily monotone.

To tell love, "Oh, come tomorrow!
Come some day, come any day!"
Is just killing

The reason why life is life.
It's just giving death advances
Which she
Never conquered. It is dying
In the saddest of all fancies.

1 2

I pine away with a longing
That makes death dearer again.
Oh, my love, why did you leave me
Without saying until when?
In my mouth, which is so lovely,
Let all joys their singing keep!
But who cares for a mad lover?
Get full of water, my eyes,
Get you full of water, weep!

Oh, my love, for whom my heart
Rings in sorrow
All its chimes!

What a lovely night this will be.

Your letter—
I've read it a thousand times.

Never change me for another!
Don't lie to me, life of mine!

I suffer so!

Whom should I tell all I suffer,
All the ills and pains that grieve me,
If you leave me?

14

I can't remember anything.

This mist of smoke will dispel
What still wanders through the air.

If I could tell you.
Oh, if I knew how to tell!

In my poor room
Everything is
Scattered about, at a loss.
Oh, who did that?
Look: António Nobre's book
Torn all across.

There's the day coming.

Oh, close, close, my weary eyes,
Green eyes that were mad and glad!

My body aches,
I feel cold.

Oh, my God, why am I sad?

And my pale hands, my long hands,
Press closely against my breast
These dead flowers whose scent clings.

Alas, love is only this!

I fall asleep.

The poor pupils of my eyes
Are just blind maidens, poor things!

1 5

Clasp me warmly, clasp me near
In the close chain of your arms,
As in that evening divine . . .

Tarry not, my love, my dear;
Darling, pity my poor sorrow,
Life of mine!

The half-light is growing darker
In the room
Where I await and await
Your coming.
My love, my dear, be not late!
The day ends in the slow gloaming.

And the roses, fainter, fainter,
Lose their petals, murmur low:
"We want him to tread upon us,
But, alas!, he tarries so . . ."

1 6

How keen the cold
Of this autumn evening!

All the day there was no sun.
The warm sun, where has it been?

Six strokes of time have this moment
From the great cathedral's bronzes
Slowly rolled,
And in the air there begins
To spread a very fine mist,
So cold!

Vague figures pass . . .
But he tarries, he is late . . .

The leaves of the scattered trees
Fall, twist and go to their fate.
Night comes in.
The mist thickens,
It involves me, cold and thin.

Why dost thou weep, dost thou tremble,
My poor heart?
My hands grow colder;
They are white like a white thing.
I don't feel them.

How keen the cold
Of this autumn evening!

And I go back to my room
As if I went to my death,
To a slow death,
Disillusioned, weary, weak . . .

A solitary tear runs down my icy cheek.

17

Who is poor is always poor,
He is poor beyond recall.
Who is rich is rich and noble
Though he be nothing at all.
This about having or not
Is nothing novel to offer.
Let us all be in the right
And know how to love and suffer.
As for all those goods and chattels,
All the things that fortune gives us
Or that labor conquers for us—
All that has no legs to stand on . . .
(This is what my life has taught me.)
I'd rather have the regret
That your long absence has brought me.

18

Be silent, promise no more!

What are your promises worth
If the doubt that you have given me
Fills all the soul to its brinks?
And our love,
In that endlessness of doubt,
Wanders derelict and sinks.

Be silent, promise no more!

Let what remains of my fondness
Become nothing, like a flower,
Which fades when they pluck it thus.

Don't speak so loud! Good-bye.

Is anyone looking at us?

Lovely, golden,
Like the moon when it awakes
In the evenings of July . . .

Her mouth,
Very small and very clear,
Was sensitive, somewhat shy,
Like the pomegranate flower;
And her eyes were very far,
In some world we do not know,
They were like two valleys
With two bright lakes of crystal down below.

Far off, in a sea of blood,
The sun dies,
And a vagueness of the wind
Makes the solemn palm trees shiver.

Damask was strewn on the floor,
Precious damask,
On the cold mosaic floor
Girt round with vases of gold.

Men swore many things that night.

And she, smiling, proud and distant,
Stood out clear, like a new goddess.

They clapped, they cried and they raved.
No one asked for wine again.

Dance, my child, dance!

Yes, I shall dance, I shall dance!

And her bodice,
In the dance,
Slipped down slowly,
Showing her two little breasts
Which were very closely tumid
Like two golden fruits of flesh.

How you dance, love, how you dance!

The veils fall, and all around
The gracefulness
Of her slight and subtle body
They seem like mists made of silk.

A great ruby idly shines,
Proud jewel, between her breasts,
Like a star.

She is almost naked,
And the dance goes on, goes on.

The Tetrarch's face
Is lined with tears and distress.

She is now dancing upon
The brocades she wore before
On her body's restlessness.

On her sex
Two emeralds shine,
Green and rare.

And the slow voice
Of the lithe dancer
Comes out distantly and lazily,
Sensual and warm in its choice:

"Prophet, whose eyes are so dark,
You will be mine this great night
Before the moon can be seen . . ."

I heard throughout yesterday
What the free sea had to say.

We wept, we laughed and we sang.
He spoke of the way he had,
Of his fate.

Then, to grow gayer, he rose
And, dancing slowly along,
He sang
A wet and lovely song.

His breath is a scent that gives
Something painful to the soul.

Waste of endless waters bare . . .
Grave of the men of my race,
When shall I lay me down there?

Then he moved away in silence
And I moved away the sadder,
Wearier than I had been.

Far off the sun's death still gleamed,
Purpling the waters that dreamed.

"Mysterious voice of the waves,
Voice of truth and voice of love,
Dying voice, wonderful voice,
Telling the sorrows I have . . .
Bitter voice of those who stay,
Trembling voice of those who go . . ."

And poets, when they sing free,
Are but echoes of the sea.

II

Curiosity

1

The most important thing in life
Is to create—to create beauty.

To do that
We must foresee it
Where our eyes cannot really see it.

I think that dreaming the impossible
Is like hearing the faint voice
Of something that wants to live
And calls to us from afar.

Yes, the most important thing in life
Is to create.

And we must move
Towards the impossible
With shut eyes, like faith or love.

2

Oh, take away the roses you have brought!

I don't want them,
Nor do I want you to ring
Again the chime
That you will always be
The real melody,
The real motive every time
Of the songs that I sing.

Both of us were quite mistaken.

Now that I know to the full
The fullest taste of your kiss,
I love you less and I feel
The fever of more than this.

Of course you don't understand . . .

Yes, yes, I'll remember you,
Though, you know, memory
Is something we can't command.

3

I am sick with weariness,
But life
Requires so much of my heart
That I say to everyone
Who is in fullness of youth:
Yes, I accept . . .
Yes, yes . . .

Renounce? Why?
Renunciation makes us weep,
And you see my eyes are dry.

4

What really hurts me,
Believe me,
Is to notice
That we hardly ever agree
When we speak about anything
That we see.

There's that slow smile of yours again . . .
It seems to say:
"Our bodies understand each other.
That is enough. Why complain?"

5

Proudly
You tell me
You have the courage to flee
From the fairest of temptations.

But
What was that flight worth,
What does that prudity afford
To anyone who uses it
And makes of it his only lord?

You grow old, like anyone else,
Withdrawing your flesh and feeling
Just as if
You gave them away in orgies . . .

Afterwards
Who will look at you?
Who is going to praise your beauty
With the ardor of their youth?
Who, in passing, will still keep

Some memory
Of certain things in your body
Which were beautiful in truth?

Oh sad ruin
Of yourself, oh unknown ruin!

Love, laugh, sing, weep!

6

Drink more wine
And put
More lipstick
On your mouth so thin and fair,
And smoke,
And lean back on the blue brocade
Of that cushion over there.

You have sometimes
A peculiar smile
Which vaunts
Of some certainty you bear,
As of someone who knows everything
And gets everything he wants.

Cigarettes, love? They're there quite plain.

What, going? . . . Where are you going?
Are you going?

When are you coming again?

7

Let the world speak!
Just smile!
No more than that.

When anyone,
Just by supposing,
Says
Something evil of ourselves,
It is because he has a dim
Notion that, in the same case,
What is appearance in us
Would be quite the truth in him.

Just a smile—no more than that.
See, I am smiling at them . . .

8

Don't stay there!
Come nearer to me!
Sit here!

Take that pout out of your mouth,
Scarlet line
In the fine
Colorlessness of your face!

Come nearer, nearer to me!

With the murmur of the waters
Of my singing
I shall make your eyelids droop.

Silence. It seemed like the sea . . .

Why tremble, love? That was nothing.
Only the wind taking up
The dead sand with a vague sound.

How your flesh burns!

Kisses . . . Oh, so many stars . . .

There comes the moon
Like clean linen for a wound.

9

Yes, I remember quite coldly.

There is no feeling at all.

But, really,
Who would have believed
If I had said
That all the love that I gave you
Was never a part of me?

If passion, or even madness,
Never once passed through our souls,
What would life be?

It's a pity, but I must not understand you.

My fancy was different—
A love
That asks nothing of the body.

This love,
Of which you speak to me, biting
Your red mouth
And caressing
A certain masculine detail
Of your body—
Look here, all that leads to nothing . . .

That sort of love
Is degrading, very vile,
It's selfish and strangely moved.

Why should that brutal thing that says "I want you"
Be a good reason why we should be loved?

The night draws in. It is colder.

I know that you are not coming.
You have lied to me once more.

The rain
Becomes dense.
The light has faded. Who loves
Never defines anything.

The rain goes on making wet
The shadows of the cold night.

This desire to kiss you
Will end by being,
Yes,
Just a tired obstinacy,
An impertinent feverishness ...

1 2

I loved. Who has never loved?
I gave myself to all pleasures.
Who denies himself that?
No pleasure ever was refused . . .
But all that is over.

When youth is past,
Comes this age they call mature.
Everything tastes of defeat.

My hair was once dimly golden,
Like the hair of so many I have kissed
And prefer, I know not why.

Not even life knows me now.

I sang once. Now I just sigh.

1 3

I have no longer any pride.
I have lost
The golden spell of my hair,
The soft, very subtle grace
Of my smile,
And the lucid wave-like motion
Of my lithe and supple body.

The very tone of my voice
Seems painful and far away,
As in a desert a river.

The pity of my decay! . . .

So much beauty lost forever!

1 4

I pity you when you say
It is my fault
That your life has gone that way.

Put that clearer:
Why is it my fault?
Oh, because I was the first? . . .
How childish you really are,
Poor boy whom I loved so gladly,
My golden boy,
Lithe body
That I used to bite so madly! . . .

I pity you when you go on like that.
Look here: life
Is always what we want of it.
Don't laugh,
Don't suppose
I am going to joke.
And if sometimes it surprises us
With one thing or another,

Believe me,
That is only
Because only very seldom
Do we affirm to ourselves
What we really want of life.

How childish you really are,
Poor boy whom I loved so gladly,
Lithe body
That I used to bite so madly! . . .

1 5

That joy that you saw in me
Was simply a nervous joy—
The false gaiety we seek
Just to show others we are gay
In the first moments
Of a great sorrow.

Yes, great sorrows are like that.
They enter deep, very deep,
Until they seem to be lost
In some place within the heart.
Not even the heart hears them call.
But
The mistake does not last long.
First
There are drops of bitter tears,
Complaints,
A vague rage.
Then resignation appears:
A smile which seems of disdain,
A smile which is very sad,
A smile which is itself pain.

16

Yes, the magnolias you have brought are very nice,
And I suppose
This means
You want a truce.
What a device!
Excuse me, but I won't accept
That part.

I am so sick of our past
That, if I could,
I would—
Yes, I would—
Break into pieces this mad heart.

That bit of linen,
Tear it up!
I've put irony everywhere.
My love was just a caprice
And I've no regret to spare.

It was a subtle caprice.

Why
Does your mouth
Try so mockingly to please?

My letter?
Oh, just a joke.
You won't read it to anyone else, will you?

Could I love you? Quite impossible!
You are handsome,
You are manly,
But I am beautiful too.

My letter! . . .

I just wrote out, like a youth,
Without thinking, on an impulse . . .

Could I love you? Never!

Am I speaking truly?
Of course I'm telling you the truth.

If all that you said just now—
A few words, no more than that—
Was all that you felt and had
To say,
Why do you wonder
That I should be sad?

You might have pitied
This illusion
Which was the greatest and fairest
Of those which have made me sigh.
Yes, you could have lied: it would
Have been so easy to lie.

I tried to kiss you? Forgive me.
You could have devised a pretext
(A pretext is not a crime):
"Not now . . . No . . . Some other day . . ."
I would have been satisfied.
But it was you—
You and your mouth and your eyes—
Which were lying all the time.

If you doubt your body can
Really tremble close to mine
And feel
The same full fleshly embrace,
Strip it fully,
Let it come into my arms
And don't speak to me,
Say nothing, nothing at all,
Because the silence of two
Gives more freedom
To the things love makes befall.

If what you see in my eyes
Is still too little
To give you a real assurance
Of this want of you that cries,
Take my life's blood,
Take all I have or can have,
If so much be necessary
For one to be understood.

1 9

Why deny me a kiss?

Your hostile unresponsiveness
Stales what in me would still find life
Worth living,
And my desire grows more with this.

Why deny me a kiss,
Lovely mouth,
Bitten flower? . . .

My sadness comes from
Your hostile unresponsiveness
And also
From that uncertain and tragic fate
Which to all of us clings,
From that unfathomable mystery
Which girds us round,
From the little that we are
In the eternal flow of things.

Why deny me a kiss?

I sought in the painful longing
That his eyes left me forever
The courage,
The firmness, the proper will
To pass quite out of his life.

Now I have become the man
Everyone wants me to be—
Sane and normal, a poor devil
Who obeys the deep convention,
The very moral convention,
Of kissing the eternal Sphinx.

I have left my love forever.
I have done what the world wants.

III

Small Sculptures

1

I seek beauty just in form,
Never
In the beauty of intention
The beauty that dieth not.

Because the bronze is well chosen
Why say
That the sculpture is well wrought?

2

Many voices
Rise and clash
And noise and confusion fall
Like a storm
On the silence of the kraal.

Then the nigger dance begins . . .

There they are—
Four marvels to tempt desire!,
Bronzes
Of the best statues of Rome.

And the dance
Begins
Once they have covered their sex
With banana leaves.

The warm moonlight is like lard
On the burning sand.

Oh, what a mad
Tropical drunkenness this weaves!

And they dance,
Singing
Some slow monotonous witch-song,
On two notes only, diabolical and sad.

One
Has the eyes of a prisoner who is in love
And the dexterity of a gladiator born.
His eyes never leave mine,
And his mouth,
Half-open in a slow smile,
Seems a fruit of fire
With silver seeds that shine.

To their hips
They have tied rattles,
Horseshoes, cattle bells,
Coins, roots,
Branches aflower,
Idols of wood,
Ivory beads, and . . .

The dance seems to have no ending . . .

I fall down tired on the sand . . .

3

Someone says we must know life
All through and in every measure.
Well, I really
Know everything, more or less.
The only thing I don't know
Is the weariness of pleasure.

4

In love—
Now don't question me!—
There were always
Two kinds of men.

This is quite true
And greater than life's self is.
No one down here can deny it
Or dismiss.

One kind of man
Looks on, without love or sin:
The other kind
Feels, grows passionate, comes in.

5

You're wrong, I tell you again.

In love
The only lie we find out in the future
Is that which seems
The best truth now,
The truth that seems to fall in with our fates.

Love never really lies:
It simply exaggerates.

6

All self-control
Brings balance into our soul
And also
A rather calm way of judging,
A truly critical state.

So we
Can easily separate
The worse from the better thing.

But just see:
How love is full of caprice!
Of everything that we wanted
To reveal and swore we would,
Only this certainty
Remains to us, all the same—
That I don't know who you are
And you don't know who I am.

7

I have tried to do without you.
How keenly
I have tried!

You think my jealousy nonsense?
Perhaps you're right.
Yes, that will fit.

But, really, in life
Everything is madness
If our heart drops into it.

8

If you want
To have silence
Round the dirty things you do
And live free,
Be evil, never be true.

Learn how to clasp your own hands
In the proper churchman's gesture;
Look down humbly
But let everyone see your posture.

Then speak slowly,
Just as if the world were to you
A false image, a bad sleep.

And, if ever you talk of death,
Sigh deeply, sigh very deep.

9

Friends, raise your glasses
And drink to love and to life!
Come, drink!
That way you'll get
To be as firm as I am.

Let the touching glasses tinkle!
We are living yet.

My tunic is slipping off.

Rose petals
Fall into my glass and freeze.

Silence. What a flesh appeal!

Who clasps me? Whose arms are these?

When I talk with you, in straying
Words, my pleasure finds its brink:
I don't think of what I am saying
And I say all that I think.

And once again
I affirm—
Deny it who ever would?—
There is no happiness
Like being just understood.

11

Let us finish.
Oh, let us finish forever.

Why go on?

Not even a kindly word,
Not a smile,
Nothing
That can please or even try . . .

No, let us finish . . .

Yes, let us finish or die . . .

1 2

A vague, cruel dissonance
Lives in the sound of your voice
When you speak of love, my own;
And when your kisses do kiss me,
Alas!, I feel it has grown.

1 3

To die young,
That is what I want!

What pleasure can there be in being old
And living uselessly in the shade
Of all deprivals, in a slough?

Oh, to die young
And with roses on my brow!

1 4

When I look at the red roses
That your garden idly shows
I think I should put on mourning
For myself because of those.

1 5

I've left off drinking, my friend.

Yes, I have set wine aside.

But if
You really want
To see me drunk—
This is between us, you see—,
Take slowly up to your mouth
The glass meant for me,
Then pass it over to me.

16

I had the heart of a friend
And it was a noble heart.
It understood all I felt
Without my having to say it.
It met
My doubts with its certainties,
And in
The worst moments of my life
It could advise me and please.
But, one day—
Oh, for everything that was!—
That great heart
Slipped from mine, fell down and broke
Like common glass.

17

Fate
Several times
Comes my way;
But
It cannot take away
The calmness that is my state.

Only
In my eyes
Some vague sadness does its duty.

I don't complain.
I don't despair.

My wish is to die in beauty.

1 8

When they say that life is short,
They're wrong, I'm ready to swear:
Though you put a great love in it,
There will still be life to spare.

1 9

Don't bear me malice, forgive me . . .
But the coldness I now put
In my kisses
Is neither fatigue nor anything.

Your body
Has the necessary charms
To deceive love or to win,
And your mouth
Has the scent of the carnations
When the night is coming in.

It is not fatigue nor anything.
It is simply an assurance
(I do not know where it comes from)
That I feel within my heart.

No, my love, you are not he
Whom my dreams often descried . . .

Love, forego reality.

Reality has just lied . . .

2 0

In the listlessness I live in
Even your disdain, if I seek it,
Can't help me, for all my trying.

In singing I pass away,

And my soul is like the swan
That sings the better when dying.

IV

Olympiads

1

The morning is full of light.

The Marathon race begins
With a sign
Given by the golden voice
Of Pindar, Pindar divine.

And those bodies
Which are sculptures
In their muscles and their grace,
Holy flesh
Without the taint
Of any woman's embrace,
Which would make it
Sick, dull, hard to understand,
Start out clear and run their way
Through the wet and tender sand.

Among many
There is one

Whose graceful motion attracts
My involuntary eyes.
He is tall, quick, nervous, free.

Silence. He won? Was it he?

Red roses, fresh and untainted,
Unstinted roses,
Are on his brow.

Women's arms are now put round him.

My soul is an artist's soul,
And a tragic certainty
Pains me deep and pains me now.

2

There the ball goes!
Go on, you! On to it!
Run,
Put your soul into the thing!
Defend it! Hold fast! What now?

And the ball, entering the goal
Suspends the muscular joy
And all these youths' happy glow.

Clapping breaks out like a storm
And the sunlight is more faint.

Then the game begins anew.
The "Reds"
Are still involving the "Lions,"
And the attack,
Close and quick,
Goes on showing who is winner
In this fair game fairly played
And worth playing with such soul.

The ball suddenly leaps
And passes—he was late!
Between the raised and unavailing arms
Of the nice boy at the goal.

Clapping, clapping . . . This is great!

Someone throws a big red rose
To the eleven that won.

And far off, in a Bohemia
Of colors, dies the slow sun.

Almost naked,
Springy,
Dark,
With a gesture
Full of litheness and of sway,
He raised the disk in his arms,
And the disk
Went off,
Nobly thrown
In a large and manly way.

In his eyes,
Very soft and very big,
An expression
Of weariness and of sin
Became keener,
Became clearer
When he noticed I was looking.

His mouth smiled
Proudly,

Condescendingly,
As does a lover who hesitates
In the gift
Of his body
When absent and far from him
To whom he had
Sworn to be true.

The day dies
In a dull light,
And the roses
Girding round the winner's brow
Begin to fade
Like a glorious trophy losing
The color that made it move.

Fair slave of strength,
Flee from love!

4

The afternoon is dull and misty.

Vague drops of rain
Fall, and the clouds
Stumble, dancing in the wind.

The sunlight,
Hesitating, very vague,
As seen in a dull blade's face,
Falls on the plain
Where I await
The beginning of the race.

Horses and horsemen
Come in a proud
Thundering way;
They appear
In a vertigo of motion
Right down there.

The light
Suddenly
Becomes a little more clear.

What a joy
In that
Splendid youth
That goes by!
And the dull and dry
Sound of the horses,
Galloping, galloping,
Gives me a big manly feeling
And a healthy sadness too.

The rain is now falling thicker,
Coming
In whirlpools,
Hard and hard.
It wets all the green grass,
It chills the crowd,
Which however does not stir
Until
The last race passes.

In spite of the showers
And of the wind,

So cold, so keen,
The fine figures of the horsemen
Play
Upon my nerves
A clarion tune
Which is sensual and is gay.

A sudden laugh,
A woman's laugh,
Bursts out
Like a breaking windowpane
That someone has leaned against.

And the effort
That I make
Not to show anybody
What I feel
Leaves me
After all
White-faced, miserable, dun.

I go out.
In the air
There is still a little sun.

5

The afternoon is just ending.

The last echoes of the band—
A dance of Aragon,
Fade away.

The afternoon,
Somehow,
Has not the natural air
Of just merging into evening.

Then he appears in the arena,
Golden flower!,
Very sensual, very manly,
And lithely
He strives to come near the bull.
The crowd
Breaks out into shouting madness.

Then,
With a supreme noble gesture,

He raises his arm
To kill.

The daylight is like a flame,
The silence is deeper still.

The horns touch the gold and silk,
And he falls,
Conquered,
Torn,
His brow all covered with blood.

The evening
Now draws in coldly and slow.

He has his belly exposed,
And the darknesses
Of his manhood
Everyone can see them now.

V

Dandyism

1

The night, slowly . . .

Out of doors
The couples
Are preparing for the dance.

"Who will dance with me?"

"I will,"
Shouts a dark Mary
With a broad and lovely face.

The harmonium,
Murmuring,
Starts the motion of the couples,
Which is yet but a slight thing.

Now
The bodies
Cling closer
In the slow and sudden shifts
Of the tune.

"Turn about! Who loves the more?
Whose love for his love is such?
Who loves most suffers the most.
I don't want to love too much."

Round the dancers
People gather
Who had been scattered about,
And my partner,
Swinging happily,
As if under
The spell of some distant dream,
Feels . . . What does she feel, I wonder.

I stop, but my arm stays
On her shoulder, round her shoulder.

The night
Is quite dark.

Oh, if only I could sing
Something no one should forget!

I think and look on in silence . . .

Lanterns are already lit.

It was that boy—that one
Who holds a flower in his mouth,
A carnation,
Red like the silk round his hips.
My glance goes
All over
The warm and flexible grace
Of the manhood that he shows.

Alas, life
Is so deceitful, so cold,
So different from that which we
Have as ours,
That it is better to desire it
As something that floats beyond
The actual life that we see.

Let us sit down there . . .
Let us rest now . . .
And, listening to the harmonium
And looking
Tiredly
At the couples out of line,
I feel exactly as if
I had been drinking some wine.

2

See with me
The dawn. It is near.
Do not go yet.

Love, love, do not part from me,
For to part is to forget!

If there be sun
I shall feel better,
Even alone, even feeling
The fear
That I may remember you
In the clinging mistiness
Of some very frail sensation
That scarce has the power to fret.

Love, love, do not part from me,
For to part is to forget!

Press me against your breast
But do not kiss me.

A kiss
Might be our death.
For death, I would rather die
In the far-off full desire
(This I feel), the one I will not
Either realize or tell.

To desire is to build, whether
This or that, or ill or well.

Come,
Be brighter, be kind!
Lift up your head,
Look me in the eyes,
Look at me, do not be afraid!

All the mystery I was
Exists no longer,
And the very common secret
I always hid, you now have it,
You take it with you. I gave it.

There's the dawn. Look, snow is falling—
White petals,
Slow,
In the dull
Cold air which seems very old.

Now
It is you who says,
"A little longer! . . ."
No, I won't stay.
Good-bye, good-bye! I feel cold . . .

3

"I'll come again soon. If not,
I'll send you word . . ."
You said that
With the full promptness of youth
When you were shaking my hand.

I doubted
And smiled to show it
So that you might understand.

Then you repeated your promise
In a nicer offhand way.

I am accustomed to doubt,
To feel that everything fails—
Alas for whoever thinks
Without letting his heart speak!
But I did try to deceive
My heart and think you would come,
That you might . . .

After all,
My doubt was the certainty,
It was my doubt that was right.

4

To go and listen to the sea
At nightfall
Is, you say,
Romantic nonsense,
Decadent rot,
And yet
You come every, every day
To listen to me,
And I
Am quite common, quite uninteresting . . .
Yet you come . . . —Why?

"Oh, you're an artist.
I couldn't miss
Listening to you,
And I could say this better
In a kiss."

Don't exaggerate!
Life
Is as funny as a grave.

You poor girl, don't try to kiss me.
Move away and just look nice.
Getting sad?
Your eyes look so.
They're wide and wild, like the eyes
Of those who lose what they get.

Don't spoil
That carnation!
Control yourself or seem like it . . .
Don't worry
Because you cannot forget.
Make your mouth shine,
Give it a smile,
Make it look like a red star!

Night is the weariness of light.
It lengthens out all dreams,
In it all things are greater—
Souls themselves are.
Like the sadness of love
It gives us
A pardon that covers all.
But I suppose you don't like it . . .

Like a boat upon the waters
Your flesh still creaks.

It is not yet just simply at the mercy
Of the echoes
Of your unforgetfulness.
It is still unweary . . .

Wait, there's the sea's voice again
With its dark and drawn-out pain . . .

To hear and to understand
The sea and its voice is grand.

Good-bye! Tomorrow, pale flower,
Come in your black dress—
That one
Which reveals
To the full
Your body
Which is frail as a wave is,
And put on
A black hat to fit with this.

Don't worry . . . Now don't stay . . .
You'll come tomorrow in black?
Yes?
. . . As on the very first day.

5

Seated in my balcony
I gaze in turns on
The night that falls and the rose
That you have put on my breast.

And, a long while
In silence,
I hear a voice that speaks to me . . .
What voice is this,
So clear, so pure,
That asks me never to question
Or lose faith in destiny?

I bend my head
And meditate
On that very high desire
That is with me
And is greater every moment . . .

In the branches of the trees
The wind
Passes and murmurs something.

The shadows fall,
Suddenly dense, in repose.

I can hardly see my hands.

At my feet
Falls the fine,
The frail body of that rose.

6

They say we don't love each other.
They even say,
With that irony of theirs,
That whenever we two meet
There is snow on the next day.

How those people are mistaken!
How those miserable people
Amuse me, though they do not!
They don't see us talk together,
No one saw us hand in hand,
They don't even know we kiss . . .
How those people are mistaken
About what we don't confess!

They say we don't love each other
For some reason or another—
Anyhow, that we don't . . .

Only your heart and my heart
Could reply . . .
They could reply but they won't.

7

Today it is I who asks you
To send me some news of you,
To say something, anything.

Tell me about yourself . . .
Forget that disdainful smile
(It really set me at ease)
When you tried so hard to kiss me.
You can see that I do love you,
But I am full of caprice.

And if that smile
Is the only thing that made you
Disappear so out of season,
Well, really, I cannot think it
A truly sufficient reason.

As soon as you rose
And, quite calm,
Stretched out your hand towards me,
And, by saying nothing,
Stressed

That farewell's cold irony,
My soul
Is sick,
Feverish, letting all things lag . . .
And my smile—that very smile—
Is drooping like a wet flag.

8

What is it that the spring murmurs?
What voice has the spring behind it?
Love, if happiness exists,
Do not say where I can find it.

It is better to go about
Desiring it
In this feverish turbulence
Which may nevertheless
Keep stagnant upon the surface;
And the contorted
Muddle
Of all that we feel awhile—
It is not difficult
To gird it all round with softness,
And to be merry—to dance,
And to look happy—to smile . . .

Indifferent to all we are
The fresh spring goes on and on.
What does it say? A song,
A prayer, a sorrow, mere music?

To have a certainty,
To inquire,
To know where,
To ask that something befall—
All that is like calling someone
Who never answers at all.

Live only at the mercy of sensation.

To define ourselves
Is simply to curtail
The soul
And to close our understanding.

And anyone who affirms
That in the strength of mere thought
Lies all greatness that can bless
Does not see that, if that were so,
He couldn't stand all its stress.

Yes, everything flows and leaves us,
And the dregs
Or the softest-winged emotion,
Of what subtlest the soul weaves,
Is like the lees
The wine
Leaves in the cask that it leaves.

And the spring
Goes on and on.
Is it, love, as
We have felt it all the time?
No.
For me
It is rather as I see it—

Water passing through wet grass.

9

There is a sigh in my life
Which at each step makes me know
The distance that separates
What I say from what I do.

Who gave it me
Has gone away.
I was left in the cold bitterness,
The interminable bitterness,
Of having to keep it
As the only way
To go on living at all.

There is a sigh in my life
Which is like a passing tear,
Which passes but never ends.
To tell it? What would I gain?
To keep it? I die of feeling it.

There is a sigh in my life
Which at each step makes me know
The distance that separates
What I say from what I do.

1 0

In your last letter
You called me decadent.
How funny!
Your letter
Made me laugh.

Was that an insult?
Well, all you managed
Was to be really kind.

Men,
Or peoples,
Heartsick
Of understanding everything,
Decay
When they cling,
Rather than to the austere pleasure
Of creating,
To the sterile, fine delight
Of seeing what is done and meditating.

(Don't let your mind wander!
Don't go away!)

And pleasure
Is quite a deep
Philosophy in itself,
Even—what are you laughing at?—
The firmest yet easiest flowing.

Now come near me.
I want to kiss you, to feel
Your brown body's burning sway . . .

You refuse? Well, I am going . . .

That's the right and proper way . . .

11

The cloud that passes,
The smile that floats,
All
That lives really and intensely,
That is eternal and brittle—
An architectural detail,
A bit of sky,
All
Has in the mirror the same weight,
The same value,
The same reality too.

Night seems to fall on my eyes.

Are you going to speak of love?
Take care! It may not be true.

1 2

In the silence
Of my sorrow's listlessness
I have been tearing up
My last illusions.

I require nothing of life.

What is it we build at all
When we give friendship or love?

Don't bother. I know quite well . . .
You were the only thing left—
A very frail cambric thread
Involving
A very solid illusion.
It went away like the others.

I require nothing of life.

To forget—that's what I choose.

And if, with scrupulous dandyism,
I work the knot in my tie,
That is still a useless fault—
One of the few I won't lose . . .

VI

Birds in a Royal Park

A PHEASANT

I fell sick with love.

It was a very blue dove,
Like heaven when the sun is seen.
I shall fly with her
From a jealous nightingale
Who likes to tease
My heart with keen
Ironical melodies.
We shall go
To that country of the mists,
To that legendary country
Where the moon hides
In the mists that darkly stand.

Oh mists, why do you gird round
Lord Byron's land?

Sometimes
I think of a page who had me
And of a king who used to kiss me

When the queen slept.
But when they told her
She hit me so much, so much,
That even the heart in me wept.

Do you hear?

There is again
The nightingale
Saying that— ...
Oh, but if there be
One single truth
In all that his melody
Seems to tell,
It will be fire on a wound,
I shall bid all this farewell.

In an old lake of old Scotland
I shall let death set me free.

THE SAD NIGHTINGALE

I asked things of all the trees.
I got so tired of just hearing
Speech with no meaning I see.
I asked questions of the stars
But I don't see that they shine.
They don't for me.

Well, just a short while
Ago
I touched a rose red like pain
And it scattered at my touch . . .

Fallen there,
It looked more like
Drops of spilt blood
Than just petals of a rose
To which my touch had been rude.

Tell me, waters of the lake:
Should I be punished for this?
Am I just misunderstood?

THE GRAY OSTRICH

They tear off my feathers
But no complaint of mine is heard.
I am a very
Well-bred bird.

If I wanted to
I could hurt
Their brown hands—
The brown hands of those
Who tear off my poor feathers.
But I really
Don't complain,
Though my body
Is being stripped
Quite plain.

And those women,
Those
Who madly use
These nice feathers that I wore
And of which they all make free—

They pass by me without looking
Or laugh if they notice me.

But no complaint of mine is heard.
I am a very
Well-bred bird.

VII

Motifs

A RAG DOLL

There was once upon a time
A very small
Rag doll.

It was very nice and pretty
But it was poorly dressed too.

In its eyes there was a sadness
Which was like an inner shade.
The sad eyes were sapphire blue
And the smile she had was like
A flower going to fade.

Near the middle
Of the shop window
Of the small shop where she lay,
That poor rag doll, that sad rag doll,
Caught no one's eyes all the day.

No one saw the smile she had.

No one even went in and asked:
What is the price of that kid?
How much does that Princess cost?

Years went by, and with them went
Everything that was my youth
And my happiness is lost.

Who will buy, at any price,
The Doll that my eyes found out
In the window of the small shop
In that small street without stir?

Who will buy her? No one, no one.

How many souls are like her!

LULLABY

Sleep, my little baby, sleep!
A noise is wandering outside.
Is it the sea or the wind?
Sleep, my boy!
                    Let it abide.

I see the stars shining clear
Through the window if I peep.
I am sad and lonely here.

And my low voice goes on singing:
Sleep! . . . Sleep! . . .

THE FADO

From a boy
All my dreams
Were to grow and to go sailing,
To be a big sailor-man.

Now
I see life must not be lived
With the passion that we want.
All fades from our poor eyes' span.

Love—who had love as I had it,
So deeply, so warmly given?
Such a desire burnt my flesh
That all those my body touched,
My body's litheness and tan—
Wander through the evening selling
Their frail sex to any man.

Alas for those who have love!
Alas for those who have none!
It's always sad, anyhow,
To long back for anyone.

Oh, I was loved!
How long
They clapped, whenever I sang,
For the longing in my song
Set in my voice
Which was warm but quite love-free.
In a tear
I used to sing
The past and present of me.

Wine
Filled the glasses.
Souls
Came to the surface
Of the talk that had no stealth.
"Let us drink our own health, boys!
Boys, let us drink our own health!"

And there was always, oh always,
The caress
Of her who sings in the shadows
The sad song of her own state
And who is ours anyhow.

Yes,
I bit mouths whose eyes were crying,
Just to bite them once again;

One day
I got married
Just to see what life was now.

Then I sail out for two years.
I leave the wife. There I go—
For my country,
To serve my country,
Like a sailor, the old way;
And these chevrons on my arm
Say all that I have to say.

I am now back, and I find
That bitch has another man.
She moans her rut with another.
I hardly know if I care.
"With another," they say, "others,"
That's what I'll say everywhere.

Alas for those who have love!
Alas for those who have none!
It's always sad, anyhow,
To long back for anyone.

VIII

Sad Songs
of Love

1

My eyes have wept, they have wept
For someone who made them weep.
Now I'll have all their tears kept
For me, and the rest may keep.
My eyes are tired of my madness.
They look on life as it is.
They go on getting less gladness
And less faith, for life is this.
They are weary, they are sad.
But things are like this. Why weep?
I'll weep—for others, how mad!
For me, and the rest may keep.

2

The earring set in your ear
Swings about when you just stir.
I should like to set a kiss
Where it touches you—just there.
There is a topaz like gold
In that earring that you own,
There is a very red ruby
And another precious stone.
How I suffer when I see
The way it has when you stir!
Oh, how I should like to kiss
Where it touches you, just there!

3

If you leave me, I'll just tell
Everyone that I left you,
For in this world of mistakes
When we lie they think it true.
You say my mouth has no longer
The power to make love be,
That it wakes no other mouth,
That your mouth is not for me.
But be careful, I am clever,
I'm too clever to be true:
If you leave me, I'll just tell
Everyone that I left you.

4

My love, when he went away,
Said no word and spoke no name.
He set his eyes on the floor.
He cried and I cried the same.
We held hands a while and knew
It was love that held them then.
But oh, the sadness that grew
From that deadly "Until when?"
A tear broke out and fell slowly.
We breathed not each other's name.
We spoke nothing, we said nothing.
He cried and I cried the same.

5

If you pass the churchyard when
I come to be buried there,
Ask the kindly earth to eat not
The curls you praised in my hair.
I do not want you to cover
With flowers my face and head,
Nor do I want you to weep
To others that I am dead.
No, don't even kiss in parting
My body, so lithe and fair.
But I should like you to keep
The curls you praised in my hair.

6

You get no more songs from me,
For I sing out of misgiving.
I am like the altar candles
Which give light and die in giving.
If only my voice a while
Might melt the coldness you show,
If only your mouth would smile!
But I am too sad, I know,
And nothing in my heart dandles
The hope that is now misgiving.
I am like the altar candles
Which give light and die in giving.

If I could make you come around
Every day, as you used to do,
To speak with me from within that lucid vision—
Strange, extremely sensual, and caustic;
If I could tell you, and you could hear me,
My poor, my wonderful, my talented artist,
What life has been—this bohemia,
Draped in rags and stars,
Infinitely sad, pedantic, counterfeit,
Ever since these eyes of mine, clouded
By tears, saw you in a coffin;
If I could, Fernando, and you could hear me,
We'd go back to the same routine: you, there where
The stars and blessed mornings
Court one another in the eternal light of a smile;
And I, here, a vagabond of unbelief
Taking my hat off to judicious men . . .

Everything around here moving along as it used to;
The same unblinking idiocy
In the men you knew
—Veritable well-spoken wretches . . .
And the same story: hours, minutes,
Nights all the same, days all the same,
Everything the same! Waking up and falling asleep
Under the same hue, on the same side, always
The same everything and in everything the same position
Of condemned men, forced to their feet to face life—
Without incentive, without faith, without conviction . . .

Poets, hear me! Let us transform
Our natural anguish from thinking
Into a dreamlike hymn!, and next to him,
Next to the exceptional comrade we now remember,
Let us remain for a few moments in song!

ACKNOWLEDGMENTS

I first met António Botto in the Robarts Library of the University of Toronto in the early 1990s. Since those years almost two decades ago, when I encountered the many editions of his poems, letters, and plays in the stacks, I've been reading and thinking about Botto as I've pursued other projects. I began to include selections of Botto's poetry in an introductory course to Luso-Brazilian literature I regularly teach. These readings with my students, together with my own extracurricular incursions into Botto's bibliography, kept Botto to some extent always present in my mind and moved events toward the present volume.

Colleagues, students, and friends have encouraged my work with their unstinting enthusiasm, questions, and gifts of information or references. Anna Klobucka provided welcome counsel at an important moment in the preparation of this project and freely shared her own work on Botto. The Toronto students who thought about Botto with me awakened perspectives and suggested interpretations. As usual, it is a pleasure to thank David Higgs, Manuela Marujo, Aida Baptista, and Ricardo Sternberg. Dr. Fátima Lopes of the Biblioteca Nacional de Portugal was generous and accommodating during one of my research stays in Lisbon. The readers for the University of Minnesota Press were helpful in their criticisms and recommendations, and, although we did not always agree, their comments identified aspects of the volume that called for clarification or further explanation. I am especially grateful to John Emil Vincent for his eloquent sensibility to the nuances of Botto's poetry and Pessoa's translations, and for his careful reading of the introduction.

The staff of the University of Minnesota Press welcomed this undertaking and brought it to fruition with habitual finesse and professionalism. It is a pleasure to thank Doug Armato again for his scholarly collegiality, and, of course, Richard Morrison, the driving force behind this and so many other ventures.

NOTES

Introduction

1. Klobucka's study explores Botto's queer public self-creation in the literary and social environments of Lisbon, including Botto's imagined connections to gay artists on an international scale. (All references in the notes appear in the selected bibliography.)

2. I use *gay* and *queer* here as a convenient shorthand and am aware that these terms acquired their contemporary meanings in later years and in different social contexts from the ones in which Botto lived and wrote. *Queer* is a term especially loaded with many possibilities of meaning, "[a] word," notes Eve Kosofsky Sedgwick, "fraught with . . . many social and personal histories of exclusion, violence, defiance, excitement" (*Tendencies* 9). In the specific context of modernism, "critics have long pointed to the pervasiveness of nonnormative desires in the making of the modern; *queer,* unlike *gay* or *lesbian,* is by definition generalizable and therefore apt to make the most of [the] atmosphere of permission" (Love, "Introduction" 744, emphasis in original). Love's essay serves as the introduction to a cluster of articles on queer modernism.

3. Translations, unless otherwise attributed, are mine.

4. Pessoa wrote several poems in English. One of them, "Antinous," is about the emperor Hadrian's grief over the death of his boy lover. This poem was published in 1918. Pessoa also wrote poetry under different literary personalities, or "heteronyms"; Richard Zenith's essay explores the possibility of a gay heteronym in Pessoa's archive.

5. Fortunately for readers of Portuguese, Eduardo Pitta has begun to reissue Botto's collected oeuvre (*Canções e outros poemas*; *Fátima*). See the selected bibliography.

6. See Almeida 69–82. For more biographical information on Botto, see Fernandes (*António Botto*); Klobucka; and Howes ("Botto, António").

7. For time lines of Botto's life, see Fernandes (*António Botto* 13–20); and Pitta (*Canções e outros poemas* 13–21).

8. Within the purview of classical Hellenic civilization, of course, homosexual relations were a standardized practice. Such practice characteristically occurred between socially unequal men and adolescent boys and was meant to be temporary as a sort of apprenticeship or mentoring. Botto's encounters, on the other hand, typically evade such characterization. The intensity of emotion and desire creates a libidinal democracy that drives the impulse toward lasting union and happiness precisely in the frequent denial of such possibility, the consequence of social sanctions against homosexuality.

9. Botto himself gestures to this experiential basis, suggesting that poetry both is born of experience and is itself a kind of experience. In the first letter of the *Cartas que me foram devolvidas* (1932), Botto writes, "I have the right to my ideas but not to my life. Of my *Canções* and my art an enormous amount has been said! I haven't even tried to explain, publicly, this or that misunderstood detail. What would explaining accomplish? . . . The poet is he who is able to take interest in the things that others disdain and don't understand. . . . Yes, my love: great verse isn't sentiment . . . great verse is experience."

10. In Joaquim Manuel Magalhães's opinion, "if we consider António Botto . . . merely as an 'aesthete,' he emerges as a ridiculous figure of mediocre writing. However, if we consider him as a thematizer of a sexual reality and as an organizer of a difficult verbal lineage, he

emerges as one of the most interesting poetic enterprises of the first half of the Portuguese twentieth century" (17).

11. Aldrich also notes that "Winckelmann's sexuality was far from foreign to his views on Greek art and society" (49).

12. Botto echoes this idea in "I have no longer any pride" where he describes the "wave-like motion" of his own "lithe and supple body." The reference eroticizes the ocean and draws it into the universe of homoerotic attraction.

13. The dancer here is Salome, who caused the execution of John the Baptist ("Prophet whose eyes are so dark"). Salome was a common theme in fin de siècle literature.

14. See the introduction and chapter 1.

15. See 141–85, especially 153.

16. See the note to "The most important thing in life."

17. See note 2, above.

18. For further comment on the emergence of gay or queer literature in modern Portugal, see Lugarinho.

19. That Botto's poetry is unprecedented and moves beyond fin de siècle eroticism is proved by the controversial critical reception of the *Canções*.

Foreword by the Translator

1. Manuel Teixeira Gomes (1860–1942) was a writer and diplomat who was president of the Portuguese Republic from 1923 to 1925.

2. *Fado* is a type of song regarded as the national musical genre of Portugal. Pessoa's equation of *fado* and prostitution is unusual. Pessoa may, in part, be implicitly referring to the legend of the prostitute Maria Severa Onofriana, who was also a *fado* singer. For a study of this legend, see Colvin.

3. António Nobre (1867–1900) was Portugal's outstanding Symbolist poet. His most well-known book of poetry is *Só* (1892). Pessoa is referring here to Botto's mention of Nobre's book in "I can't remember anything."

4. Pessoa has "tore it across" in the typescript.

I. BOY

1. "NO, LET US KISS, ONLY KISS"

A version of this poem, titled simply "Canção" (Song), appears in the page proofs of what was to have been the fourteenth issue of *Contemporânea* (1929), the magazine in which the literature of Sodom controversy began. (The page proofs of *Contemporânea 14* were reproduced in facsimile in 2005; see the selected bibliography.) In the 1929 version of this poem the fifth line reads "Teu frágil corpinho loiro" (Your frail little golden body) instead of "Teu viril corpo trigueiro" (Your manly body so brown), the line that appears in the 1930 and subsequent editions of *Canções*. In the *Contemporânea* proofs the tenth and eleventh lines read "Que bem ficam as rosas / Nos teus cabelos doirados!" (How well the roses look / In your golden hair!). In the 1941 and subsequent editions, Botto modified the fourth line to read "Para outro momento" (For another moment).

6. "WHO IS IT THAT CLASPS ME TO HIM"

In the introductory remarks to the 1922 edition of the *Canções*, Teixeira de Pascoaes (the nom de plume of Joaquim Pereira Teixeira de Vasconcelos, founder of the literary movement known as *saudosismo*) singles out this poem as one of the few in which it is possible to find "the living and unadorned voice of the poet's blood and soul."

9. "I AM GLAD, I REALLY AM"

As it appears in the 1922 edition of the *Canções,* this poem bears the dedication "Eternecidamente—a Fernando Pessoa" (Tenderly—to Fernando Pessoa).

10. "NO, THIS ISN'T JEALOUSY"

The verb that Pessoa translates as "like" (in the line "Have you not liked me so often?" in stanza five) is in the original Portuguese *gostar* (*de*). This verb is unambiguous in its meaning here as "to take sexual pleasure (in)."

11. "YOU SAY YOU'RE COMING, AND THEN"

In the fourth line, *pink* is used as a noun (for carnation).

14. "I CAN'T REMEMBER ANYTHING"

See the note on António Nobre for Pessoa's "Foreword," above. In addition to *Só,* three other collections of Nobre's poetry were published, posthumously: *Despedidas* (Farewells, 1902), *Primeiros versos* (First verses, 1921), and *Alicerces* (Foundations, 1983).

II. CURIOSITY

1. "THE MOST IMPORTANT THING IN LIFE"

The dedication of *Curiosidades estheticas* (1924) is "À Memória Bela de Walter Pater" (To the beautiful memory of Walter Pater). This poem immediately follows.

14. "I PITY YOU WHEN YOU SAY"

The poet and translator Edward A. Lacey (1937–1995) published a translation of this poem, which is, to my knowledge, the only other English translation of any of Botto's poems apart from Pessoa's. See Leyland 647.

Pessoa's translation of this poem imbues it with racist overtones evident to a modern sensibility but not entirely present in Botto's original. This may be the result of Pessoa's own exposure to such ideas as a boy in South Africa, and to the fact that both Botto and Pessoa lived during the era of Portuguese colonialism in Africa, which eventually ended in 1975. What Pessoa calls "the nigger dance" in line 6 is *batuque* in Portuguese, an indigenous African dance. For Botto's *senzala*, the living quarters of slaves on sugar plantations, Pessoa uses the Afrikaans word *kraal*, derived from the Portuguese *curral* (pen or enclosure for livestock).

One of several individual books of poetry incorporated into the *Canções, Olympíadas* was first published separately in 1927. In that book, and in all succeeding editions of the *Canções*, beginning with the 1930 volume, *Olympíadas* bears the following inscription, not translated by Pessoa: "A todos esses jovens que ao sol e á chuva, num campo, durante horas inteiras,—quase nús, cultivam com uma formosa animalidade inconsciente, a alegria muscular na destreza dos desafios" (To all those youths who, on a field in rain or in sun, for hours on end—almost nude, with a beautiful, unconscious animality—cultivate muscular joy through the prowess of their contests).

Pindar (c. 518–428 BCE) was a Greek lyric poet who wrote odes in praise of the Olympic games and their winners. His poetry celebrates male athletic prowess.

In *Olympíadas*, this poem is dedicated to Álvaro de Campos, one of Pessoa's heteronyms. The reference to the "dance of Aragon" is to the *jota aragonesa*, a traditional dance from the region of Aragón in northeastern Spain.

VIII. SAD SONGS OF LOVE

The poems in this section first appeared in the 1930 *Canções*. Botto there dedicates them to his wife, "À Carminda de todo o coração" (To Carminda, with all my heart).

To the Memory of Fernando Pessoa

"À Memória de Fernando Pessoa" was published for the first time in the 1941 *Canções*. It occupies its own separate subsection, titled "Poema de Cinza" (Ash poem).

SELECTED BIBLIOGRAPHY

The Works of António Botto

Entries in each section are arranged in chronological order. This bibliography is not exhaustive.

LETTERS

Cartas que me foram devolvidas. Lisbon: Paulo Guedes, 1932. (2nd ed. Lisbon: Argo, 1940.) The *Cartas* also appear in the 1941 and 1956 editions of the *Canções.*

MANIFESTO

O meu manifesto a toda a gente. [Lisbon]: Tip. Anuário Comercial, [1921?].

NOVEL

Isto Sucedeu Assim . . . Lisbon: Argo, 1940.

POETRY

Trovas. Lisbon: Bertrand, 1917.
Cantiga de saudade. Lisbon: Bertrand, 1918. (I have been unable to verify the existence of these first two entries in the standard bibliographic sources; see Fernandes *António Botto,* 125.)
Cantares. Versos de António Botto; músicas de Nicolaŭ d'Albu-

qŭerqŭe Ferreira; illŭstrações do pintor António Carneiro. Lisbon: Anuário Comercial, 1919. (2nd ed. Sassetti, 1928.)

Canções do sŭl. Estudo sobre o livro *Canções do sŭl* por Jayme de Balsemão. Lisbon: Centro Tipográfico Comercial, 1920.

Canções. Lisbon: Libánio da Silva, 1921.

Canções. Segŭnda edição mŭito aŭgmentada com ŭm retrato do auctor, palavras de Teixeira de Pascoaes e novas referencias por Jayme de Balsemão. Lisbon: Olisipo, 1922.

Motivos de belleza. Lisbon: Portugália, 1923. (Contains a "Notícia" by Fernando Pessoa.)

Curiosidades estheticas. Com palavras de Junqueiro, um retrato do auctor, e outras referencias valiosas. Lisbon: Libánio da Silva, 1924.

Piquenas esculpturas: ultimas canções. Lisbon: Anuário Comercial, 1925.

Olympíadas: canções. Lisbon: Anuário Comercial, 1927.

Dandysmo: canções. Lisbon: Anuário Comercial, 1928.

Anthologia de poemas portuguezes modernos. Ed. António Botto and Fernando Pessoa. Lisbon: 1929.

Canções. Edição definitiva de toda a obra poética do autor acrescentada de alguns inéditos e com palavras do grande escritor e artista Manoel Teixeira Gomes antigo chefe de estado. Lisbon: Anuário Comercial, 1930.

Canções. Nova edição definitiva de toda a obra poética do autor com oito canções inéditas e um estudo crítico de Teixeira Gomes antigo chefe de estado. Lisbon: Paulo Guedes, 1932.

Ciúme: canções. Lisbon: Momento, 1934.

Baionetas da morte. [Lisbon]: Anuário Comercial, 1936.

Os sonetos de António Botto. Lisbon: Baroeth, 1938.

A vida que te dei. Lisbon: Fernandes, 1938.

As canções de António Botto: obras completas. Lisbon: Tipografia Henrique Torres, 1940[?]. Privately printed.

As canções de António Botto. Nova edição. Lisbon: Bertrand, 1941.

Antologia de poemas portugueses modernos. Ed. Fernando Pessoa and António Botto. Coimbra: Nobel, 1944.

O livro do povo. Lisbon: Ecléctica, 1944.

Ódio e amor: poemas. Lisbon: Ática, 1947. (Two separate editions of this book exist, with different covers. One contains a photo of Botto and an introductory note by Fernando Pessoa, which is an extract from his essay "António Botto e o ideal estético em Portugal.")

Poesia nova: poemas. Primeiro volume. [São Paulo? 1949?]. Privately printed. With a cover design attributed to Picasso.

Fátima: poema do mundo. Aprovado por sua eminência o senhor cardeal patriarca de Lisboa D. Manuel Gonçalves Cerejeira. Rio de Janeiro: 1955.

As canções de António Boto. Nova edição definitiva. Lisbon: Bertrand, 1956.

Ainda não se escreveu. Lisbon: Ática, 1959.

As canções de António Botto. Com um estudo crítico de Fernando Pessoa. Obras completas de António Botto I. Lisbon: Ática, 1975.

Canções. [Lisbon]: Círculo de Leitores, 1978.

As canções de António Botto. Com um estudo crítico de Fernando Pessoa. Lisbon: Presença, 1980.

As canções de António Botto. Lisbon: Presença, 1999.

Canções e outros poemas. Ed. Eduardo Pitta. Vila Nova de Famalicão: Quasi, 2008.

Fátima. Ed. Eduardo Pitta. Vila Nova de Famalicão: Quasi, 2008.

Bagos de prata: antologia poética. Ed. Marcelo Tápia, Luis Dolhnikoff, and João Carlos de Carvalho. São Paulo: Olavobrás, n.d.

Canções. N.p.: Agartha, n.d.

STORIES

Os contos de António Botto. Nova ed., aumentada e definitiva. Lisbon: Bertrand, 1915. (Several editions/printings of the collected stories of Botto were published. Only a few are listed here.)

O meu amor pequenino. Porto: Lello; Lisbon: Aillaud & Lellos, 1934.

Dar de beber a quem tem sede: contos para crianças e adultos. Coimbra: Atlântida, 1935.

A verdade e nada mais: antologia infantil de alguns contos do autor. Coimbra: Coimbra Editora, [1935].

Não é preciso mentir. Porto: Editora Educação Nacional, 1939.

Os contos de António Botto, para crianças e para adultos, neste segundo volume das obras completas está incluído "O Livro das Crianças" que foi aprovado oficialmente para as Escolas da Irlanda pelo Ministério da Educação Nacional dêsse país e também muitas páginas inéditas juntaram nesta obra de acentuado carácter social educativo. Porto: Latina, 1942.

A guerra dos macacos: contos ilustrados. Lisbon: Empresa Literária Universal, 1943.

Regresso (novelas inéditas). São Paulo: Clube do Livro, 1949.

Os contos de António Botto. 8th ed. Lisbon: Bertrand, n.d.

Ele que diga se eu minto. Lisbon: Romero, n.d.

Histórias do arco da velha: antologia de contos infantis. Ed. António Botto. Lisbon: Minerva, n.d.

Os olhos do amor e outros contos. Lisbon: Minerva, n.d.

PLAYS

Alfama. Lisbon: Paulo Guedes, 1933.

António. Novela dramática. Lisbon: Anuário Comercial, 1933.

As comédias de António Botto. Terceiro volume das obras completas e primeiro do teatro. Lisbon: Romero, 1945.

9 de Abril: teatro em três actos. Lisbon: Francisco Franco, n.d. (A draft
of this play is included in *Motivos de belleza* 41–130, with the note
that it was written toward the end of 1919.)

*Teatro: Flor do mal, Nove de Abril, Aqui que ninguém nos ouve, Al-
fama.* Porto: Centro Editorial Português, 1955[?].

Translations

POETRY

Les cançons: antologia. Trans. Gabriel de la S. T. Sampol. Muro:
Ensiola, 2004. (Catalan)

Lieder. Trans. Sven Limbeck. Heidelberg: Elfenbein, 1997. (Ger-
man)

Songs. Translated from the Portuguese by Fernando Pessoa. N.p:
1948.

STORIES

The Children's Book. Trans. Alice Lawrence Oram. Illus. Carlos Bo-
telho. Lisbon: Bertrand, n.d. (Contains a "Short Biography of
António Botto.")

Critical Studies and Other Works

Aldrich, Robert. *The Seduction of the Mediterranean: Writing, Art,
and Homosexual Fantasy.* London: Routledge, 1993.

Almeida, L. P. Moitinho de. "António Botto, Fernando Pessoa, ou-
tros e eu." In *Fernando Pessoa: No cinquentenário da sua morte,*
69–82. Coimbra: Coimbra Editora, 1985.

Almeida, São José. *Homossexuais no Estado Novo.* Porto: Sextante,
2010.

Anselmo, Manuel. *Soluções críticas*. Coimbra: Imprensa da Universidade, 1934.

Balsemão, Jayme de. "Palavras sobre o artista e sobre o livro *Canções*." In *Canções*, António Botto, v–xiv. Lisbon: Libánio da Silva, 1921.

Bouças, Edmundo. "António Botto e as espessuras do esteta." *Metamorfoses* 5 (2004): 195–204.

Callón Torres, Carlos Manuel. "Notas para a re-leitura dum maldito: a cultura homossexual n'*As canções de António Botto*." *Lusorama* 47–48 (2001): 59–78.

Carvalho, Amorim de. *Através da obra do Sr. António Botto (análise crítica)*. Porto: Simões Lopes de Domingos Barreira, 1938.

Cavafy, C. P. *Collected Poems*. Trans., ed. Daniel Mendelsohn. New York: Knopf, 2009.

Cidade, Hernani. "Tendências do lirismo contemporâneo. Do 'Oaristos' às 'Encruzilhadas de Deus.'" *Boletim de Filologia* 5 (1938): 199–228.

Colvin, Michael. *The Reconstruction of Lisbon: Severa's Legacy and the Fado's Rewriting of Urban History*. Lewisburg, Penn.: Bucknell University Press, 2008.

Contemporânea 14. Ed. José Augusto França and Carlos Ventura. Porto: Invicta Livro, 2005.

Fernandes, Maria da Conceição. *António Botto—um poeta de Lisboa: Vida e obras: novas contribuições*. Lisbon: Minerva, 1998. (See 125–34 for an additional bibliography of Botto's work.)

———. "António Botto, também jornalista." *Jornal de Letras, Artes, e Ideias* 728 (September 1998): 38–39.

Higgs, David. "Lisbon." In *Queer Sites: Gay Urban Histories since 1600*. Ed. David Higgs, 112–37. London: Routledge, 1999.

Howes, Robert. "Botto, António." In *Who's Who in Gay and Lesbian*

History: From Antiquity to World War II. 2nd ed. Ed. Robert Aldrich and Garry Wotherspoon. London: Routledge, 2002.

Howes, R. W. "Fernando Pessoa, Poet, Publisher, and Translator." *British Library Journal* 9 (1983): 161–70.

Klobucka, Anna M. "António Botto's Impossible Queerness of Being." In *Portuguese Modernisms: Multiple Perspectives on Literature and the Visual Arts.* Ed. Steffen Dix and Jerónimo Pizarro, 110–21. Oxford: Legenda, 2010.

Klobucka, Anna M., and Mark Sabine. "Introduction: Pessoa's Bodies." In *Embodying Pessoa: Corporeality, Gender, Sexuality.* Ed. Anna M. Klobucka and Mark Sabine, 3–36. Toronto: University of Toronto Press, 2007.

Lancastre, Maria José de. "Pessoa e Botto: análise de uma mitografia." In *E vós, Tágides minhas: miscellanea in onore di Luciana Stegagno Picchio.* Ed. Maria José de Lancastre, Silvano Peloso, and Ugo Serani, 393–404. Viareggio (Lucca): Baroni, 1999.

Leal, Raul (Henoch). *Sodoma divinizada: Uma polémica iniciada por Fernando Pessoa, a propósito de António Botto, e também por ele terminada, com ajuda de Álvaro Maia e Pedro Teotónio Pereira, da Liga de Acção dos Estudantes de Lisboa.* Ed. Aníbal Fernandes. Lisbon: Hiena, 1989. (This source includes a reprint of Leal's 1923 booklet on pages 73–88 of this volume, as well as other documents related to the literature of Sodom polemic.)

Leyland, Winston, ed. *Gay Roots: Twenty Years of Gay Sunshine: An Anthology of Gay History, Sex, Politics and Culture.* San Francisco: Gay Sunshine Press, 1991.

Love, Heather K. "Forced Exile: Walter Pater's Queer Modernism." In *Bad Modernisms.* Ed. Douglas Mao and Rebecca Walkowitz, 19–43. Durham, N.C.: Duke University Press, 2006.

———. "Introduction: Modernism at Night." *PMLA* 124.3 (2009): 744–48.

Lugarinho, Mário César. "Al Berto, In Memoriam: The Luso Queer Principle." In *Lusosex: Gender and Sexuality in the Portuguese-Speaking World.* Ed. Susan Canty Quinlan and Fernando Arenas, 276–99. Minneapolis: University of Minnesota Press, 2002.

Magalhães, Joaquim Manuel. "António Botto." In *Um pouco da morte,* 17–20. Lisbon: Presença, 1989.

Maia, Álvaro. "Literatura de Sodoma: o Sr. Fernando Pessoa e o ideal estético em Portugal." Reprinted in Leal, *Sodoma divinizada,* 53–68.

Mateus, Margarida Maria Alves Nabais. "Relações literárias entre Fernando Pessoa e António Botto." Master's thesis, New University of Lisbon, 1999.

Ministério da Cultura. *António Botto, 1897–1959.* Lisbon: Biblioteca Nacional, 1999. (See 81–87 for an additional bibliography of Botto's work.)

Monteiro, Arlindo Camillo. *Amor sáfico e socrático: Estudo médico-forense.* Lisbon: Instituto de Medicina Legal de Lisboa, 1922.

Monteiro, Maria da Encarnação. "Pessoa tradutor." In *Incidências inglesas na poesia de Fernando Pessoa,* 57–74. Coimbra: 1956.

Nemésio, Vitorino. "Canção: À maneira e à memória de António Boto." *Colóquio/Letras* 113–14 (1990): 5–12.

Nogueira, Albano. *Imagens em espelho côncavo (ensaios).* Coimbra: [Gonçalves], 1940.

Pater, Walter. *The Renaissance: Studies in Art and Poetry. The 1893 Text.* Ed. Donald L. Hill. Berkeley: University of California Press, 1980.

Pereira, Paulo Alexandre. "*O desvio e o preço*: Régio, leitor de Botto." In *Centenário de Branquinho da Fonseca: Presença e outros percursos.* Ed. António Manuel Ferreira, 147–64. Aveiro, Portugal: Universidade de Aveiro, 2005.

Pessoa, Fernando. "António Botto e o ideal estético creador." In *Apreciações literárias: bosquejos e esquemas críticos*, 107–130. Aveiro, Portugal: Estante, 1990. (This essay was first published in the 1932 edition of the *Cartas que me foram devolvidas*.)

———. "António Botto e o ideal estético em Portugal." 1922. In *Textos de crítica e de intervenção*, 119–33. Lisbon: Ática, [1993].

———. "Crítica a 'Ciúme,' de António Botto." 1935. In *Textos de crítica e de intervenção*, 217–22. Lisbon: Ática, [1993].

———. *Obra poética*. Ed. Maria Aliete Galhoz. Rio de Janeiro: Nova Aguilar, 1983.

Pindar. *The Complete Odes*. Trans. Anthony Verity. Oxford: Oxford University Press, 2007.

Pitta, Eduardo. "Uma cegueira consciente." In *Canções e outros poemas*, António Botto. Ed. Eduardo Pitta, 23–38. Vila Nova de Famalicão: Quasi, 2008.

———. *Fractura: A condição homossexual na literatura portuguesa contemporânea*. Coimbra: Angelus Novus, 2003.

Portugal, Francisco Salinas. *O Texto nas margens: ensaios de literaturas em língua portuguesa*. Santiago de Compostela: Laiovento, 1997.

Régio, José. *António Botto e o amor*. Estudos de José Régio. Porto: Progredior, 1937.

———. *António Botto e o amor seguido de críticos e criticados*. Porto: Brasília, 1978.

Sales, António Augusto. *António Botto: real e imaginário*. Lisbon: Livros do Brasil, 1997.

Saslow, James M. *Pictures and Passions: A History of Homosexuality in the Visual Arts*. New York: Viking, 1999.

Schukowski, Stefan. "Disguised Homoerotics: Subversive Strategies in António Botto's *Canções*." In *Resisting Texts*. Ed. Brigitte

Rath and Stefan Schukowski. Munich: Meidenbauer, forthcoming.

Sedgwick, Eve Kosofsky. *Between Men: English Literature and Male Homosocial Desire*. New York: Columbia University Press, 1985.

———. *Tendencies*. Durham, N.C.: Duke University Press, 1993.

Sena, Jorge de, ed. "António Botto." In *Líricas portuguesas*. Vol. 1, 65–87. Lisbon: Edições 70, 1984.

Simões, João Gaspar. "A fatalidade na poesia de António Botto." In *O mistério da poesia: ensaios de interpretação da génese poética.* 2nd ed., 169–95. Porto: Inova, 1971.

———. *História da poesia portuguesa das origens aos nossos dias, acompanhada de uma antologia*. Vol. 3. Lisbon: Empresa Nacional de Publicidade, [1955].

Taylor, Keith. "A Distant Pleasure." Review of *C. P. Cavafy: Collected Poems* and *C. P. Cavafy: The Unfinished Poems*, trans., ed. Daniel Mendelsohn. *Boston Review* (November/December 2009). Accessed on the Web, 16 December 2009. http://bostonreview.net/BR34.6/taylor.php

Teixeira, Judith. *Poemas: Decadência, Castelo de Sombras, Nua, Conferência de Mim*. Ed. Maria Jorge and Luis Manuel Gaspar. Lisbon: Edições Culturais do Subterrâneo, 1996.

Vincent, John Emil. *Queer Lyrics: Difficulty and Closure in American Poetry*. New York: Palgrave, 2002.

Woods, Gregory. *A History of Gay Literature: The Male Tradition*. New Haven, Conn.: Yale University Press, 1998.

Zenith, Richard. "Fernando Pessoa's Gay Heteronym?" In *Lusosex: Gender and Sexuality in the Portuguese-Speaking World*. Ed. Susan Canty Quinlan and Fernando Arenas, 35–56. Minneapolis: University of Minnesota Press, 2002.

INDEX OF FIRST LINES

ANTÓNIO BOTTO (1897–1959) was a Portuguese poet who wrote during the Modernist period in Portugal and published more than thirty volumes of poetry, short stories, and plays in his lifetime. In 1947, he immigrated to Brazil and died there in an accident.

FERNANDO PESSOA (1888–1935) was a poet, literary critic, and translator and is widely considered among the most important literary figures of the twentieth century. His many collections of poetry and writings include *The Book of Disquiet* and *A Little Larger Than the Entire Universe: Selected Poems.*

JOSIAH BLACKMORE is professor in the Department of Spanish and Portuguese at the University of Toronto. He is author of *Moorings: Portuguese Expansion and the Writing of Africa* (2009) and *Manifest Perdition: Shipwreck Narrative and the Disruption of Empire* (2002) and editor of C. R. Boxer's *The Tragic History of the Sea* (2001), all published by the University of Minnesota Press.